PLATONIC LEGACIES

SUNY SERIES IN CONTEMPORARY CONTINENTAL PHILOSOPHY

Dennis J. Schmidt, editor

PLATONIC LEGACIES

JOHN SALLIS

STATE UNIVERSITY OF NEW YORK PRESS

"Daydream," previously published in *Revue International de Philosophie*, vol. 52, no. 205 (October 1998), pp. 397–410, is reprinted here as chapter 3 with permission.

Published by
State University of New York Press, Albany

Printed in the United States of America

For information, address the State University of New York Press,
90 State Street, Suite 700, Albany, NY 12207

Production, Laurie Searl
Marketing, Susan Petrie

Library of Congress Cataloging-in-Publication Data

Sallis, John, 1938–
Platonic legacies / John Sallis.
p. cm. — (SUNY series in contemporary continental philosophy)
Includes bibliographical references and index.
ISBN 0-7914-6237-4 (alk. paper) ISBN 0-7914-6238-2 (pbk.: alk. paper)
1. Plato. 2. Plato—Influence. 3. Platonists. I Title. II. Series.

B395.S24 2004
184—dc22 2003068664

10 9 8 7 6 5 4 3 2 1

For Nancy

With Gratitude

CONTENTS

ACKNOWLEDGMENTS

To the Alexander von Humboldt-Stiftung and the Fulbright Commission I am grateful for the fellowships that allowed me to prepare this book during an extended stay in Freiburg in 2002–03. I am grateful also to the *Revue Internationale de Philosophie*, to the *Graduate Faculty Philosophy Journal*, and to Indiana University Press for permission to draw upon previously published papers. Thanks also to Nancy Fedrow and to Ryan Drake for their generous and expert assistance.

Boalsburg
February 2004

INTRODUCTION

LEGACY DOES NOT GO unconsidered in the Platonic dialogues. Almost the entirety of the long first part of the *Theaetetus*, ostensibly addressed to the identification of knowledge as perception, is engaged with the legacy of Protagoras. Socrates introduces this legacy as saying in a somewhat different way what Theaetetus has just declared, that knowledge is perception. The legacy consists in the maxim that declares human beings to be the measure of all things. Socrates cites the maxim in its precise formulation, and then, immediately, he asks Theaetetus: "Surely you've read that?"[1] Theaetetus assures Socrates that he has read it often, and this affirmation serves to confirm how thoroughly it is a legacy that is at issue here, indeed something passed along not just by word of mouth but also by dissemination through writing. It is not long before Socrates extends this legacy, in fact to such an extent that it comes to coincide with virtually the entire legacy of Greek philosophy and poetry, with the sole exception of Parmenides and his followers. Socrates says: "And about this let all the wise in succession except Parmenides converge, Protagoras and Heraclitus, and Empedocles, as well as the topmost poets of each kind of poetry, Epicharmus of comedy and Homer of tragedy" (152e).

Yet what counts most is the capacity to receive the legacy, or rather to take up whatever within it is genuine and true. A bit later

1. *Theaetetus* 152a. All subsequent references to Platonic dialogues are given in the text. Translations are my own, though I have consulted Allan Bloom's translation of the *Republic* (New York: Basic Books, 1968), Seth Benardete's translation of the *Theaetetus* (Chicago: University of Chicago Press, 1984), and the translation of the *Phaedo* by Eva Brann, Peter Kalkavage, and Eric Salem (Newburyport, MA: Focus Publishing, 1998).

in the dialogue Socrates tells Theaetetus that he will join him in "searching out the hidden truth of the thought of a renowned man, or rather, of renowned men" (155e). As they set out on this search, Socrates advises Theaetetus to look around and make sure none of the uninitiated (ἀμύητος) or unmusical (ἄμουσος) are listening, none of those crude persons incapable of apprehending anything except what they can grasp with their hands. Taking up a legacy requires the capacity to see the unapparent, the mysteries (τὰ μυστήρια), and this is why it can be supposed that what Protagoras told his disciples in private was quite different from what he said publicly to the many. Yet now it is solely a matter of legacy: at the time of the conversation in the *Theaetetus*, Protagoras is dead, and indeed it is mentioned that Callias is "the guardian of his things" (165a), the one appointed to look after his legacy.

Parmenides and his disciples are the only ones excluded from the expanded Protagorean legacy. In the *Theaetetus* Socrates recalls his youthful meeting with Parmenides, whom he describes with the Homeric phrase "as awesome to me as uncanny [αἰδοῖός τέ μοι δεινός τε]" (183e). He forgoes taking up the Parmenidean legacy ("so I'm afraid that we'll fail as much to understand what he was saying as we'll fall far short of what he thought when he spoke" [184a]). It is, then, hardly less wondrous that when, by common consent, Socrates, Theodorus, and Theaetetus meet early the next day at the same place, the Parmenidean legacy is literally brought to the scene in the person of the Eleatic Stranger. In the conversation that follows, this legacy is taken up, but not just in the sense of repetition or refinement; rather, at the risk of being charged with patricide, the Stranger submits the Eleatic legacy to rigorous critique and transformative appropriation. Without this critical appropriation of the Eleatic legacy, the Platonic legacy would have been unthinkable.

▼ ● ◆

In this history of philosophy since Plato, in what today one calls the history of metaphysics, critical appropriation of the Platonic legacy never ceases, not even if and when that history reaches a certain end. Yet in the ever recurrent appropriation, the Platonic legacy is repeatedly reconstituted. Thus it assumes various and disparate guises. It is pluralized so thoroughly that there could be little hope of recovering any unity other than the reference back to the Platonic texts; and even the ways in which this reference would be carried out and made binding would be so various and disparate that one would still be left with a manifold of Platonic legacies.

Heidegger underlines the enormous role that the Platonic legacy in its various guises has played in the history of philosophy from Plato to Nietzsche, that is, in the history of metaphysics. In a late essay he writes: "Throughout the entire history of philosophy Plato's thinking remains, in its various forms, decisive [*massgebend*]. Metaphysics is Platonism. Nietzsche designates his philosophy as inverted Platonism."[2] From Plato to Nietzsche there are only forms of Platonism, various and disparate forms, to be sure, and finally, with Nietzsche, a form in which Platonism is stood on its head, in which, as Heidegger says, "the most extreme possibility of philosophy is attained" and its end thus reached.[3]

Metaphysics is Platonism—nothing but Platonism, or at least nothing quite separable from Platonism, from the Platonic legacies. The studies gathered here under this title are intended to supplement this equation. Yet only in a few cases will they do so by showing how Platonism is intrinsic to the work of thinkers within the span of metaphysics. The most conspicuous—though already extreme—case is the discussion of Nietzsche's Platonism, his manifold Platonism. Augustine will, to be sure, be taken up in connection with the question of time, but more with a view to the legacy he passes along than to the legacy taken over from earlier Platonism. In addition, the "old quarrel between philosophy and poetry" (*Rep.* 607b), already thus a legacy when taken up into Platonism and made integral to its legacy, will be portrayed as it is variously resumed in the relation between tragedy and philosophy that a recent study has shown to be decisive for the history of post-Kantian German philosophy.

Granted that, with the qualifications required, metaphysics is Platonism, the question to which these studies are more persistently addressed is whether the equation can be reversed, whether, mathematically speaking, the relation is commutative. Can one say that

---

2. Martin Heidegger, "Das Ende der Philosophie und die Aufgabe des Denkens," in *Zur Sache des Denkens* (Tübingen: Max Niemeyer, 1969), 63.

3. Ibid.

Platonism is metaphysics? Or are there not moments within certain Platonic legacies that exceed metaphysics? One such moment, decisive for Plotinus, is expressed in the Platonic phrase ἐπέκεινα τῆς οὐσίας (beyond being).[4] Still more decisive for these studies is the recovery of that moment in the *Timaeus* that goes under—among others—the name χώρα and that, called a third kind (τρίτον γένος) alongside what will be called *intelligible* and *sensible*, both escapes and disrupts the governing order of the Platonism that is metaphysics. Thus, in these studies, which draw on the recovery of the χώρα, it will be a matter, for instance, of inscribing chorology within the Platonic discourse on politics, an inscription promised in reverse at the outset of the *Timaeus* yet, despite the political frame of the dialogue, not realized. Through such an inscription it becomes possible to rethink the difference between the paradigmatic city and the actual city, to show that they differ in a sense that is irreducible to a difference of sense.

In these studies it will be a matter also of attempting, ever so cautiously, to open communication between the two exorbitant moments, the χώρα and the beyond of being. And it will be a matter of inscribing chorology in Plotinian hyperontology, thereby enabling discourses on the temporality of the one and on the spacing of the one. It will be a matter, too, of opening communication between this most archaic moment of Platonism and the spacing that—as *Dasein* or *Zeit-Raum*—becomes decisive in Heidegger's venturing of another beginning over against the first—that is, Platonic—beginning. It will be a matter finally of nature, of thinking nature outside the nature beyond nature (the nature of nature) to which it was—except at the most exorbitant moments—consigned, but from which it can be freed by giving heed to choric and elemental spacings.

▼ ● ◆

All these studies deal with Platonism and its legacies, though with decided emphasis on the archaic or exorbitant moments that lie, for the most part concealed, within these legacies. To this extent the studies have a common focal point around which they—each in its

4. The phrase comes from *Rep.* 509b.

own way—circle. And yet, their figure is not that of a set of concentric circles but rather of a set of ellipses all sharing one focal point, but not both. For while these studies are all addressed to the Platonic legacies, they also engage, one by one, a series of contemporary philosophers, engage them not primarily as interpreters of Plato or of Platonism but as philosophers who address the Platonic legacies from out of their own thought. An alternative figure by which to represent each of these studies would be that of an elongated right triangle: in each case it is a matter of a dialogue that I would carry on with one of these others about a common theme, Platonic legacies. If one then imagined eight such triangles sharing the elongated side, or better, if one simply imagined the triangle rotating through 360°, the cone thus generated would provide an appropriate figure of the entire set of studies. The circumstances of the various dialogues differ considerably. In some cases, as with Derrida, Scott, and Schmidt, it is a continuation of dialogue long since under way; or of dialogue only begun or at least cut short, as with Heidegger and Schürmann; or of dialogue limited to the texts of such authors as Nietzsche and Arendt. Yet in every case what orients and energizes the dialogue is the manifold of Platonic legacies and, above all, the fecund endowment that these legacies offer to thinking today, our Platonic legacy.

CHAPTER 1

NIETZSCHE'S PLATONISM

TWO PROPER NAMES. Even if modified in form and thus conjoined.

As such they broach an interval. The various senses of this legacy, of Nietzsche's Platonism, are figured on this interval.

The interval is gigantic, this interval between Plato and Nietzsche, this course running from Plato to Nietzsche and back again. It spans an era in which a battle of giants is waged, ever again repeating along the historical axis the scene already staged in Plato's *Sophist* (246a–c). It is a battle in which being is at stake, in which all are exposed to not being, as to death: it is a γιγαντομαχία περὶ τῆς οὐσίας. As the Eleatic Stranger stages it, the battle is between those who drag everything uranic and invisible down to earth, who thus define being as body, and those others who defend themselves from an invisible position way up high, who declare that being consists of some kind of intelligibles (νοητά) and who smash up the bodies of the others into little bits in their λόγοι, philosophizing, as it were, with the hammer of λόγος.

Along the historical axis, in the gigantic interval from Plato to Nietzsche, the contenders are similarly positioned for the ever renewed battle. They, too, take their stance on one side or the other of the interval—again, a gigantic interval—separating the intelligible from the visible or sensible, τὸ νοητόν from τὸ αἰσθητόν. Those who station themselves way up high are hardly visible from below as they wield their λόγοι and shield themselves by translating their very position into words: μετὰ τὰ φυσικά. And yet, the history of metaphysics is not just their history: partly of course because their history is one of contention with the others, with those who continue to drag the invisible, intelligible kinds of things down to earth; but also because the nonmetaphysics of these others remains always a temptation to those above, just as those down below are bound sometimes to experience—even as they are captivated by such a word as *empiricism*—the attraction of the heights. For these reasons the battle has continued, has continually been renewed, its outcome remaining undecided.

And yet, finally, with Nietzsche it seems that the battle has come to an end. From the Platonic beginning, from that inaugural staging, the history of metaphysics would have run its course, coming to its end at the moment when Nietzsche, the last metaphysician, confounds beyond hope the very interval at stake throughout that history. What was way up high is cut loose and drifts out of sight. There is no longer anything to drag down to earth, and in a sense nothing is required in order to remain true to the earth—nothing except the utmost insistence on the surface that remains once the gigantic interval is no more and the sensible has been twisted free of the intelligible.

Retrospecting, one will see that Platonism casts its shadow across the entire interval running from Plato to Nietzsche. And even should one seek, beginning with Nietzsche, to step out finally into the light, one would perhaps only discover how persistently one is drawn back into the shadow; or rather, one would perhaps discover that Platonism, even as it seems to come to its end, is like a question mark so black, so monstrous, that it casts shadows on anyone who ventures to inscribe it.[1] Even at the limit, even beyond the limit, Platonism would perhaps prove not to have been left behind. Least of all by Nietzsche.

It is a question, then, not just of the interval as such but rather of various figures of movement across the interval. One figure concerns the reach of Platonism; it is the figure of Platonism as it reaches across the entire interval, decisively determining Nietzsche's thought, indeed to such an extent that, as Nietzsche himself recognizes, his thought remains a kind of Platonism. A second figure is that of the extension of Platonism

---

1. The passage being adapted here comes from *Die Götzen-Dämmerung*: "A *revaluation of all values*, this question mark so black, so monstrous, that it casts shadows on anyone who sets it down" (*Werke: Kritische Gesamtausgabe*, ed. Giorgio Colli and Mazzino Montinari [Berlin: Walter de Gruyter, 1969], VI 3: 51). All further references to Nietzsche's texts are given according to the volume and page number of the Colli-Montinari edition.

within the interval, short of the decisive break that Nietzsche ventures; this is Platonism as Nietzsche takes it to have persisted after Plato, or rather, as it was repeatedly reconstituted and passed along, the Platonism that came to inform and deform Christianity. A third figure is that of Nietzsche's interpretive move back across the interval, his turn to the Platonic texts themselves, or rather to these texts as mediated by the doxographical and philological traditions. Beyond these interpretations, found in Nietzsche's early Basel lectures, there is still another turn to Plato, one that grows out of Nietzsche's thinking, an opening to a Platonic thinking anterior to virtually all Platonism. This fourth figure thus traces an encounter beyond doxography, a turn—in Nietzsche's phrase—to "the *concealed* history of the philosophers" (VI 3: 257).

Figured thus on the interval broached by the two proper names, these four figures determine the senses of Nietzsche's Platonism.

▼ ● ◆

The first figure is that of Platonism as it decisively determines Nietzsche's thought, making that thought a kind of Platonism. This connection with Platonism is by no means something that went unremarked by Nietzsche. On the contrary, it is a bond that Nietzsche recognized, affirmed, and expressed from the earliest phase of his thinking up through his final creative year. Thus in one of the early sketches for *The Birth of Tragedy*, Nietzsche writes: "My philosophy an *inverted Platonism*: the further removed from true being, the purer, the more beautiful, the better it is. Living in *Schein* as goal" (III 3: 207). Here the word *Schein* is used to name that semblance or appearance that Platonism distinguishes from "true being." From the time of this early sketch (1870–1871), Nietzsche's strategy is to mix up what is way up high and what is down below, to invert the opposition, the interval, that Platonism would enforce, thus to regard *Schein* as the purer, the more beautiful, the better and to demote what Platonism calls "true being" to the inferior position. Even in this earliest phase Nietzsche's philosophy would arise as an inversion that comes to celebrate *Schein*.

This celebration of *Schein* is a decisive moment in *The Birth of Tragedy*. It is in reference to "the beautiful shining of the dreamworlds [*der schöne Schein der Traumwelten*]" (III 1: 22) that Nietzsche thematizes the Apollinian considered as a natural artistic energy anterior to the advent of the human artist. In the Apollinian state images shine; as in dreams, they shine forth as figures or shapes in which one takes immediate delight. When Apollinian art arrives on the scene, it comes in imitation of the protoartistic natural state; in Apollinian art, as in dreams, everything is gathered around the beautiful shining of images. Even when the Apollinian is yoked together with Dionysian ecstasy in Greek tragedy, it is the shining image that Nietzsche continues to celebrate. Tragic art is, in turn, set over against the Socratic demand for unlimited uncovering; and, as thus opposed to the force released through Socrates, it cannot but have succumbed to the Socratism that Nietzsche takes to have determined the further course of Western thought and art. As long as Socratism remains in force, the Apollinian can at best—as in Euripides—only be reconstituted as "the cool, paradoxical *thoughts*" accompanying the "fiery *affects*" that replace Dionysian ecstasies (III 1: 80). Only when Socratism comes to its self-recoiling end is the space again freed for the advent of Apollinian *Schein* and for the celebration that would invert Socratism (rethought as Platonism) and raise *Schein* above "true being" itself.[2]

This inversion and the radical dislocation that issues from it are at the core of Nietzsche's *Twilight of the Idols*, written in his last creative year, its Preface dated 30 September 1888, barely over three months before Nietzsche's final breakdown in Turin. Subtitled "How One Philosophizes with a Hammer," this text sounds out "eternal idols"—that is, everything linked to Platonism—by touching them with a hammer as with a tuning fork. Here, too, it is the hammer of λόγος that is at work (the final section is entitled "The Hammer Speaks"); what it tells primarily is the history of an error, that is, of Platonism, yet it tells this history as one by which the error came to be exposed, tells it as the story of "How the 'True World' Finally Became a Fable" (VI 3:74–75). This history Nietzsche reduces to a series of stages, precisely the stages by which Platonism came finally to be inverted and dislocated.

It was Heidegger who first recognized the decisiveness of the passage in which Nietzsche relates this curious history of Platonism as error. Indeed Heidegger marked it as the passage where, if ever, Nietzsche exceeds the Platonism that otherwise, as he merely inverts

2. This interpretation of *The Birth of Tragedy* is developed in *Crossings: Nietzsche and the Space of Tragedy* (Chicago: University of Chicago Press, 1991).

it, continues to control his thought. Since Heidegger focused attention on the passage, interpretation after interpretation has been layered on it.[3]

The passage and the history it relates begin with the true world; not yet set in the quotation marks that enclose it in the title of the passage and in the fifth, penultimate stage of the history, it is accorded at least the status of a signified, even in a curious sense that of something actual. Nietzsche says that in the beginning the true world is "relatively sound, simple, convincing"; for it was "attainable for the wise, the pious, the virtuous man,—he lives in it, *he is it.*" His very elevation, his assumption of this superior position, defines the true world, brings it about. This is why Nietzsche says that the true world is—at the beginning—a rewriting, a transcripton (*Umschreibung*), of the sentence "I, Plato, *am* the truth."

Beginning with the second stage, deferral comes into play. After Plato the true world—its name still significant, still free of qualifying punctuation—becomes such that it is unattainable for now, though promised to those wise, pious, virtuous men who formerly lived in it and were it. This stage is marked, then, by separation, by the promise of presence that is also the denial of presence. There is no longer just the wise, pious, virtuous man but also another, one that is absent but promised. Of this other that the true world has become, Nietzsche says also that it becomes finer (as if covered by a fine veil, for instance), that it becomes more compromising or trickier (*verfänglicher*), and that it becomes impossible to grasp. One could say perhaps that the true world becomes elusive and seductive. Writing in italics, Nietzsche says—as if to say all this in a single word—"*it becomes woman* [sie wird Weib]." Dropping the italics, he adds: "it becomes Christian." Here—at this stage but also, even more, in what Nietzsche says of it—so many things are juxtaposed, not to say mixed up: deferral (with its structure of promise and denial), seductive elusiveness, woman, Christianity, even sin (Nietzsche quotes: the true world is for "'the sinner who repents'"). Within the story this witches' brew is

3. See Martin Heidegger, *Nietzsche* (Pfullingen: Günther Neske, 1961), 1:231–242; also Jacques Derrida, *Éperons: Les Styles de Nietzsche* (Paris: Flammarion, 1978), 59ff.; and my *Delimitations: Phenomenology and the End of Metaphysics*, 2nd ed. (Bloomington: Indiana University Press, 1995), 160–62.

not to be analyzed but stirred and allowed to brew. But lest it be thought that here Nietzsche lays a trap by setting out an idea or essence (or whatever it will later be called) of woman, one should note that it is precisely the opposite that is under way here: it is with the appearance of the woman that the idea as such begins the recession that will culminate in its disappearance and abolition.

The drift continues. The true world, assuming next its Kantian guise, proves not just unattainable but unpromisable; there remains only the indemonstrable thought of it, effective only as an imperative. Still further: it is unknown and as such cannot even obligate, ceases entirely to be effective. Nietzsche describes this fourth stage: "Gray morning. First yawn of reason. Cockcrow of positivism"—leaving it as though it were unproblematic *only* (one would presume) because reason (*Vernunft*) has been so thoroughly problematized in the immediately preceding section of the text. In this section, entitled "'Reason' in Philosophy," Nietzsche charges reason with everything from dehistoricizing and mummifying life and becoming to falsifying the testimony of the senses and being utterly duped by language. He concludes that reason "has constructed the 'true world' out of contradiction to the actual world"; now Nietzsche encloses the true world in quotation marks, reduces it to a mere signifier. And finally, the very distinction "between a 'true' and an 'apparent' " world is declared merely a symptom of "*décadence*," of "*declining* life."

The awakening of reason can be, then, only a stage on the way to its abolition. The next, penultimate stage marks such a point: the true world has become a useless and superfluous idea, hardly even an idea but only words returning to themselves, only the "true world." Whatever it may be or not be, Nietzsche declares: "let us abolish it!" The brightness of day lets one see "Plato's embarrassed blush."

So, finally, at noon, at the "moment of the shortest shadow," at the moment when even the shadow of Platonism would finally recede, one would step out into the light. With the true world abolished, reduced to the "true world"—to something merely said, merely told, a fable—it is only a question of what world remains. Nietzsche's answer: none—for "*with the true world we have also abolished the apparent one* [die scheinbare]." No longer determinable by opposition to the true world, turned, as it were, out of this opposition, twisted free of it, *die scheinbare Welt* is now to be interpreted, not as the inferior

Erscheinung of a deferred and deferring world beyond, but in its very shining forth to sense. In this sense of sense linked to sense, it is to be celebrated as *Schein*.

▼ ● ◆

The second figure is that of Platonism short of the Nietzschean inversion, Platonism as it persisted despite being progressively exposed and compromised in that history that Nietzsche tells as the history of an error. It is the figure of Platonism as it consolidated itself outside of and over against that history, persisting at the stage that, in that history, is only one stage removed from the Platonism of Plato. Initially and for some time this figure is identical with Christianity, "Platonism for 'the people'" Nietzsche calls it (VI 2: 4). It is the advocate of declining life, of all that is weak and base—in the words of *The Antichrist*: "Christianity has sided with all that is weak and base, with all failures; it has made an ideal of whatever *contradicts* the instinct of the strong life to preserve itself" (VI 3: 169). Born out of hatred of life, Christianity invents a god who enforces this resentment, who exemplifies this contradiction of life: "God degenerated [*abgeartet*] into the *contradiction* of life, instead of being its transfiguration and eternal Yes!" (VI 3: 183).

In Nietzsche's final texts the polemics become ever more strident, the hammer of λόγος ever harder. And it becomes then ever more imperative to hear also the words in which Nietzsche celebrates life, to counter the negativity with his jubilant yes-saying.

In the second figuration, Platonism proved hardly insular. It was only a matter of time before this Platonism, reconfigured as Christianity, seeped back into philosophy as it had, at least for a while, run its course somewhat apart (with the Preplatonic philosophers, especially Heraclitus, and with "a few skeptics" [VI 3: 176]). For Nietzsche the title of that seepage is theology, and it has long since spoiled everything. Again the words of *The Antichrist*: "It is necessary to say whom we consider our antithesis [*als unsern Gegensatz*]—the theologians and whatever has theologians' blood in its veins—our whole philosophy" (VI 3: 172).

But there is also another kind of transfer from this figure of Platonism, a monstrous translation that in a certain sense enables philosophy rather than spoiling it. In *Beyond Good and Evil* Nietzsche broaches this translation: "It seems that all great things first have to bestride the earth in monstrous and frightening masks in order to inscribe themselves in the hearts of humanity with eternal demands" (VI 2: 4). It is the struggle against this Platonism in its monstrous guise—what Nietzsche calls simply "the fight against Plato"—that, as he declares, "has created in Europe a magnificent tension of the spirit the like of which had never yet existed on earth." It is this tension that energizes even the Nietzschean inversion, so that, as he says, "with so tense a bow one can now shoot for the most distant goals" (VI 2: 4f.).

The tension that has been generated lies in the very relation to truth as such—that is, in the unconditional belief in the value of truth, in the unlimited will to truth. It is precisely the tension that reaches its extreme at the moment when the belief in the value of truth impels the believer finally to put this very value in question. This is the moment in which one can no longer forgo asking whether in the perspective of life itself a higher value might not belong rather to deception and lies, whether truth itself—what one would take to be truth *itself*, secured in its alleged distinctness from its opposite—might not turn out to be only a certain kind of lie required by a certain kind of living being. This is the moment in which the unlimited will to truth—this "eternal" demand inscribed in the hearts of humanity—comes finally to demand the truth about truth itself. It is the moment in which Platonism, as advocate of truth itself, coils up at the limit and recoils upon itself. Yet, at this limit where one might expect the monstrous and frightening masks to fall away revealing truth itself, there occurs instead a releasing of the monstrosity of truth, a releasing of truth into its monstrosity.

In his skirmishes with this Platonism, Nietzsche frequently conflates it with Plato, with what the proper name would signify. As when, in the *Twilight of the Idols*, he charges Plato with being "preexistently Christian" (VI 3: 149). Or, again, in *The Gay Science*: "even we knowers of today, we godless antimetaphysicians still take *our* fire, too, from the flame that is thousands of years old, that Christian faith, which was also the faith of Plato, that God is the truth, that truth is divine." He continues, pressing toward the limit: "But what if this should become more and more unbelievable, if nothing should prove to be divine any more unless it were error, blindness, lies—if God himself should prove to be our most enduring lie?—"(V 2: 259).

There can be little doubt but that such conflation of Plato with Platonism in this figuration is largely stategic. For Nietzsche was keenly aware of a range of differentiations that set the author of the dialogues quite apart from this Platonism. This awareness is most directly and extensively attested in Nietzsche's early Basel lectures on this other Platonism, the Platonism of the dialogues.

▼ ● ◆

In 1995 the full text of Nietzsche's lectures on Plato was published in the Colli-Montinari edition (II 4: 1–188).[4] These lectures were first presented in the Winter Semester 1871–1872, a little more than two years after Nietzsche, still in his mid-twenties, had been appointed to a professorship in classical philology at the University of Basel. Initially entitled "Introduction to the Study of the Platonic Dialogues," the lectures were repeated under various titles in the Winter Semester 1873–1874, in the Summer Semester 1876, and in the Winter Semester 1878–1879, Nietzsche's last before resigning from his position at the University of Basel. The lectures thus span almost the entire Basel period and, in terms of Nietzsche's published works, extend from the period in which he prepared and published *The Birth of Tragedy* up through the year in which the first volume of *Human, All-Too-Human* appeared.

The lecture course falls into two main parts. In the first Nietzsche deals with recent Plato literature and with Plato's life and then goes on to give a summary account of each of the individual dialogues. The second main part offers a thematic presentation of Plato's thought.

In the introductory paragraphs preceding the first part Nietzsche provides some general remarks that serve to orient the entire lecture text. First of all, he declares that Plato has always—and rightly—been considered the genuine philosophical leader or guide for the youth. This vocation is linked to the paradoxical image presented by Plato. Nietzsche describes it as "the image of an overabundant philosophical nature that is just as capable of a grand intuitive vision of the whole

4. An abridged text of these lectures was published in vol. 19 of *Werke* (Leipzig: Alfred Kröner Verlag, 1913), 235–304.

as of the dialectical labor of the concept." Nietzsche says: "The image of this overabundant nature kindles the drive to philosophy; it arouses θαυμάζειν [wonder], which is the philosophical πάθος" (II 4: 7).

From this opening it is already evident, then, that what Nietzsche designates here by the name Plato is quite remote from the Platonism with which, as noted, he will later often conflate it. As an overabundant philosophical nature who arouses wonder in the youth, Plato is anything but the avatar of Platonism for the people, of Platonism configured as Christianity. On the other hand, Nietzsche does mark, at the very outset of his lectures, a connection between Platonic thought and Kantian idealism. Plato's theory of ideas—his *Ideenlehre*, as Nietzsche calls it—is said to have been invaluable preparation for Kantian idealism, since it presents already the properly conceived opposition between the thing-in-itself and appearance. On the one hand, then, Nietzsche binds Platonic thought to the later history of metaphysics; and yet, if one observes that, within the context of *The Birth of Tragedy*, Kant and Schopenhauer are precisely the thinkers who force to its limit the drive to truth and prepare thereby a rebirth of art, then the bond of Platonic thought to Kantian idealism can equally well be regarded as setting Plato at the limit of metaphysics, as bringing his thought into proximity with the Nietzschean inversion.

Nietzsche stresses Plato's talent as a prose writer. He grants, too, that Plato displays great dramatic talent. Yet he insists that it is not Plato the writer that is primary but rather Plato the teacher. The writer is only a specter (εἴδωλον) of the teacher, and his compositions only a remembrance (ἀνάμνησις) of the speeches held in the Academy. As—one might venture to say—Nietzsche the teacher of classical philology is only a specter of Nietzsche the thinker, and his lectures on Plato only an anticipation of his later encounter with Plato's thought as such.

Nietzsche turns to the recent Plato literature. Among the various scholars he discusses, two bear significantly on Nietzsche's reading of Plato. One is Tennemann, a Kantian whose works on Greek philosophy, including a four-volume presentation of Plato's philosophy, were well-known to the German Idealists.[5] Nietzsche mentions, in

5. See, for example, F. W. J. Schelling, "*Timaeus*" *(1794)*, ed. Hartmut Buchner (Stuttgart-Bad Constatt: Frommann-Holzboog, 1994), 28, 74; also Hegel's critical remark in his Berlin lectures on the history of philosophy: "The great Tennemann is gifted with too little philosophical sense to be able to grasp the Aristotelian philosophy" (*Vorlesungen über die Geschichte der Philosophie*, Teil 3, ed. P. Garniron and W. Jaeschke [Hamburg: Felix Meiner, 1996], 64f.).

particular, Tennemann's view that Plato has a "double philosophy," that is, an overt and a covert philosophy; Tennemann thus gives renewed prominence to the ancient distinction between the exoteric and the esoteric Plato, between the philosophy found in the dialogical writings and that of the unwritten teachings.

A very different emphasis was brought by the other scholar, the philosopher and theologian Friedrich Schleiermacher. What Schleiermacher stresses in his well-known Introduction to his translations of the dialogues is that in Plato's work form and content are inseparable, that alongside Plato the philosopher there is also Plato the artist. While Nietzsche acknowledges Plato's artistic talent, he nonetheless takes issue with Schleiermacher as regards the significance of the artistic element in the dialogues: Nietzsche insists on ascribing only secondary significance to Plato the artist and to the dialogues as artworks. Nietzsche declares that the intent of the dialogues is to capture actual, remembered conversations; yet rather than just realistically reproducing a conversation, Plato proceeds in a manner analogous to that of a Greek sculptor, who idealizes the figure in reproducing it. Still, it is not the idealizing, not the artistic reshaping, that is primary. Nietzsche says, without qualification: "A dialogue is not intended to be regarded as something dramatic but, in the form of remembrance, as a dialectical course" (II 4: 14). Much later in his lectures Nietzsche will insist even more strongly on limiting the import of the dramatic element in Plato's work, declaring, for instance, that "Plato's dramatic power has been astonishingly overrated" (II 4: 161).

Nietzsche turns to an extended discussion of Plato's life, drawing on a wide range of sources including, as most important, the Platonic *Letters*. Two points especially deserve to be mentioned. The first arises in Nietzsche's discussion of the course of Plato's education: Nietzsche stresses the importance of Plato's poetic tendencies, noting that Plato is said to have composed dithyrambic poems in his youth but later to have burned his poems. Secondly, Nietzsche takes care to set Plato somewhat apart from the other Socratic philosophers who persisted in the Socratic way after the master's death. On the one hand, Plato idealized the image of Socrates, while, on the other hand, his Socratic tendency was limited by his earlier Heracliteanism. Nietzsche says of Plato: "He was initially a Heraclitean and was never purely Socratic" (II 4: 45).

Nietzsche's accounts of the individual Platonic dialogues are largely summary in character. Yet even as such some of the accounts are remarkably astute, even by the standards of the best recent scholarship. For example, in his account of the *Timaeus*, Nietzsche's interpretation of the long-disputed passage on the blending of the world-soul corresponds closely to that of such more recent and very differently oriented interpreters as A. E. Taylor and Serge Margel:[6] like these interpreters, Nietzsche distinguishes between the two stages of the blending and recognizes that what results from the two elements mixed at the first stage then becomes a third component to be mixed with these same two elements at the second stage of the blending. On the other hand, it cannot be denied that Nietzsche's accounts sometimes stray from the language of Plato's texts, replacing what the texts say with traditional formulations that cannot but cover up much of what is at issue, formulations that in effect project back upon the Platonic texts a language and a conceptuality that became possible only as a result—only in the aftermath—of what was achieved in those texts. For example, in his account of the *Timaeus*, there is a passage that refers unmistakably to what in the dialogue itself is called (among its many names) the *receptacle* (ὑποδοχή) and, untranslatably, the χώρα. But when Nietzsche draws the distinction between the receptacle and intelligible being, he does so by characterizing the former as a primitive matter (*primitive Materie*) alongside the ideas, as a μὴ ὄν (nonbeing) that would have no part in the eternity of the ideas. And yet, in the *Timaeus* itself the receptacle is never designated by the word ὕλη (matter), a word that indeed plays almost no role at all in Plato's thought.[7] In the *Timaeus*, too—quite contrary to Nietzsche's account—the receptacle is said to partake of the intelligible even if in a most perplexing way; and it is explicitly said to be everlasting (ἀεί) (see *Tim.* 51a–b, 52a–b). It is perhaps, then, no accident that Nietzsche feels compelled to return to this issue at the very end of his lectures, to return in a reading more attentive to the Platonic text.

There are incisive remarks about other dialogues too. Noting that the theme of the *Phaedo* is "the philosopher and death" or "the charming away of the fear of death," Nietzsche remarks that "death is

6. See A. E. Taylor, *A Commentary on Plato's Timaeus* (Oxford: Oxford University Press, 1928), 109ff.; and Serge Margel, *Le Tombeau du Dieu Artisan* (Paris: Les Éditions de Minuit, 1995), 82.

7. The conflation of χώρα and ὕλη is found already in Aristotle (*Physics* 209b) and is frequently repeated by later interpreters. See my discussion in *Chorology: On Beginning in Plato's "Timaeus"* (Bloomington: Indiana University Press, 1999), 151ff.

the authentic inspiring genius of philosophy." Without death there would hardly be any philosophizing. Humans alone are certain of death; but there is a remedy, a medicine, that works against the effects of this certainty. Nietzsche uses here the word *Heilmittel*, presumably translating φάρμακον, which means also poison and is the word used in the *Phaedo* to designate the potion given to Socrates. The pharmacological remedy consists, says Nietzsche, of "metaphysical insights, the core of all religions and philosophies." He suggests that this connection between death and philosophy is genuinely Platonic, not Socratic. He mentions, too, that Plato's theory of immortality caused a great stir, and he notes that it was ridiculed by comedy (II 4: 85–87).

The *Symposium* Nietzsche links, predictably, to the *Phaedrus*, not only, however, as regards the common theme but also as regards the question of rhetoric. In the *Symposium* a rhetorical superiority is demonstrated by the presentation of seven speeches on the same theme as those in the *Phaedrus*, of which there are three, only one of which however went uncensored. Nietzsche concludes: "It is completely false to believe that thereby Plato wanted to present various wrong tendencies: they are all philosophical λόγοι and all true, with ever new sides of the one truth" (II 4: 104–106).

Nietzsche's brief remarks on the *Sophist* are much less venturesome than one would have hoped in view of the pertinence of several of the themes of this dialogue to subsequent developments in Nietzsche's thought. Perhaps the most notable of these themes are the determination of being as δύναμις and the enacting of the γιγαντομαχία περὶ τῆς οὐσίας. In fact Nietzsche does refer to the latter, though not by this name, when he remarks: "The passage is famous in which the εἰδῶν φίλοι and the materialists are discussed." Nietzsche insists that the former are not to be identified with the Megarians; he suggests that probably Plato had in mind "the supporters of his older view," which set the immovable ideas over against "that which they animate." Nietzsche marks the contrast: in the *Sophist* the ideas are apprehended, not as immovable, but as moving and moved (*als bewegender u. bewegter*) (II 4: 134–36).

The thematic presentation of Plato's thought that Nietzsche offers in the second main part of his lecture course proceeds with only minimal reference to the Platonic texts. Many of the interpretations border on the conventional, and one cannot but suspect that they are controlled as much by the doxographical and philological traditions as by Plato's texts themselves. It is most remarkable that Nietzsche's interpretation of Plato could have remained within such narrow bounds during the very time when, in *The Birth of Tragedy*, Nietzsche was breaking in the most radical manner with the view of Greek culture handed down by Winckelmann, Goethe, and the entire tradition of German Hellenism. Over against the narrow limits within which Nietzsche's interpretation of Plato is bound, one recalls the image of Prometheus unbound that appeared on the original title page of *The Birth of Tragedy*.

Nietzsche's thematic presentation begins with an account of the Platonic ideas, an account presented with a straightforwardness that precludes letting what is at issue in this regard reflect back upon the very nature and possibility of giving an account. Nietzsche begins with the concept, with conceptual determination (*Begriffsbestimmung*), and, first of all, identifies the ideas as the objects of such conceptual determinations. He continues with a second, enumerated point: "Objects of general conceptual determinations are not sensible things but rather another kind of beings [*eine andere Gattung des Seienden*]." He concludes with a third point intended to explain the second: "The reason for separating the ideas from the sensible is that he saw the sensible in perpetual flux and change and therefore did not regard it as an object of knowledge; but, with Socrates, he held that the ethical was conceptually knowable" (II 4: 149). Here the interpretive schema merely extends that of the previous account: it is a matter of an initial Heracliteanism that declares everything sensible to be in flux but that is then tempered by the Socratic insistence on the ethical as knowable, hence as escaping the perpetual flux of the sensible, hence as, in Nietzsche's words, another kind of beings. Nietzsche adds that just as our particular sense-perceptions correspond to particular objects so likewise must our general concepts correspond to objects that are just as unchangeable as the concepts themselves. Little wonder that Nietzsche observed, at the very beginning of his lectures, that "the theory of ideas is something very astonishing" (II 4: 7)! But what is perhaps most astonishing is that such an account could have been given, with scarcely a hint of a question, by one who during this very same period could write in the text "On Truth and Lies in a Non-moral Sense" that "truths are illusions that one has forgotten are such, metaphors that have been used up and that have lost their sensible force, coins that have lost their image and now come to be considered no longer as coins but as metal" (III 2: 374f.).

Nietzsche insists repeatedly on the priority that the ethical had for Plato. Thus in positing the ideas Plato's point of departure was the good, the beautiful, the just, and his aim was to shelter these ethical abstractions from the thoroughgoing flux of the sensible. Nietzsche grants that it would be possible for one to posit the ideas on the basis of a consideration of the visible world, but he insists that Plato did not proceed in this way, that the genesis of the theory of ideas did not lie in a consideration of the visible world. The origin of the theory is not aesthetic; the ideas are not posited on the basis of aesthetic contemplation or intuition. Thus Nietzsche returns to a point on which he insisted earlier: that Plato's artistic drive is secondary and is thoroughly governed by another drive, the moral. As Nietzsche says of Plato: "He is an ethicist through and through" (II 4: 161). From this point Nietzsche moves rapidly to a string of conclusions—that the body is the prison of the soul, that the task of philosophy is to seek release from the sensible—that point unmistakably to the metamorphosis of Plato's thought into the Platonism for the people that will become the principal target of Nietzsche's genealogical critique. As to Plato himself, the author of the dialogues, one would do well at this point to heed what Nietzsche confesses in a note penned in 1887: "Plato, for example, becomes in my hands a caricature" (VIII 2: 187).

Yet, as noted already, Nietzsche returns at the end of his lectures to a discussion of what the *Timaeus* calls the receptacle, the χώρα. As before, the word *matter* (*Materie*) is brought into play, along with *foundation* (*Grundlage*) and *raw material (Rohstoff)*. But now, noting that it was Aristotle who called it ὕλη, Nietzsche puts in play—as almost nowhere else in the lectures—the precise, if paradoxical, language of Plato's text. He mentions that its apprehension is of such a character as to be hardly trustworthy (μόγις πιστόν). And he notes, remarkably, that "because it is always the same as itself and unchangeable, it insinuates itself in an illegitimate way . . . into the realm of the νοητά [the intelligibles]." Then, finally, most remarkably, Nietzsche calls it by the names that it is given at the heart of the Platonic discourse, and accordingly he indicates one of the most decisive and controversial issues at the center of the *Timaeus*: "Difficulties arise from the fact that Plato also calls it χώρα and ἕδρα and calls the becoming in it a becoming ἔν τινι τόπῳ [in some region or place]. Greatly contested question whether the so-called matter is perhaps nothing other than space" (II 4: 185f.). Nietzsche is at the threshold of some of the most decisive demands imposed by Plato's discourse on the χώρα, perhaps most notably that of thinking together, as one and the same, the enclosedness of a receptacle and the free openness of what will come to be called space.

▼ ● ◆

There is still a fourth figure of Nietzsche's Platonism. It is the figure of a turn to Plato in a dimension quite different from that governing Nietzsche's Basel lectures, a turn determined less by bonds to the doxographical and philological traditions than by Nietzsche's rare capacity to discern the most decisive ambiguities and the incessant circulation of thought within these ambiguities. It is through this turn, above all, that Nietzsche encounters Plato's thought in a way that opens toward its singularity rather than dissipating its force in the transition to Platonism. Precisely in this turn the caricature of Plato would be undone for the sake of what one would call Plato himself, were not the image that emerges so driven by ambiguity as to threaten the very propriety of the proper name.

Indeed there are moments even in the Basel lectures when Nietzsche takes care to complicate what would otherwise come down to a caricature. Thus Plato the Heraclitean is not said simply to become Socratic instead; nor is Plato the artist consistently presented as having been transformed without remainder into the Socratic moralist. To be sure, Nietzsche stresses in the lectures that Plato's artistic drive came to be limited by the moral impetus received from Socrates. To be sure, as Nietzsche writes in *The Birth of Tragedy*, Plato "burned his poems that he might become a student of Socrates." And yet, Nietzsche continues, "where unconquerable propensities struggled against the Socratic maxims, their power, together with the impact of his monstrous character, was still great enough to force poetry itself into new and hitherto unknown channels. An example of this is," says Nietzsche, "Plato" (III 1: 80f.). Even if he destroyed his poems, he did not cease to write, did not become one who, like Socrates, does not write. No doubt, had he not come under the spell of Socrates, he would have written entirely otherwise; in *Human, All-Too-Human* Nietzsche even ventures that "It is no idle question whether, if he had not come under the spell of Socrates, Plato might not have discovered an even higher type of philosophical man who is now lost to us forever" (IV 2: 220). Yet, even under the spell of Socrates, Plato persisted in writing; he remained an artist.

In an early text entitled "The Greek State," one of his *Five Prefaces to Five Unwritten Books*, Nietzsche underlines the struggle, the ambiguity, that remained: "That he excluded the genial artist from his state was a rigid consequence of the Socratic verdict on art, which Plato had made his own in a battle against himself" (III 2: 270f.). Yet this battle against himself did not cease when Plato made the Socratic verdict on art his own; rather it was precisely then that it reached its highest pitch, that it became most intense. With this image of Plato battling against himself, with this image of dynamic but also energetic ambiguity, Nietzsche touches on the singularity of Plato's thought.

There are other passages, superb ones, that open toward this singularity, passages in which Nietzsche draws the image of one who, with enormous artistic endowments, encounters the force of the Socratic verdict and injunction and is set in perpetual battle against himself, divided from himself and yet set turning, circulating, within the ambiguity.

As when, in *Beyond Good and Evil*, which declares Plato's to be "the greatest force any philosopher so far has had at his disposal" (VI 2: 114), Nietzsche poses as a physician in order to ask: "How could the most beautiful growth of antiquity, Plato, catch such an illness? Did the wicked Socrates corrupt him after all? Could Socrates have been the corruptor of youth after all? And did he deserve his hemlock?" (VI 2: 4).

Or as when, again in *Beyond Good and Evil*, Nietzsche writes of Plato's secrecy, of the concealment in which he holds back, hiding himself; and of his sphinx nature, as if he were destined to present the riddle to tragic man; and of what, above all, had led him, Nietzsche, to dream about Plato's secrecy and sphinx nature. Here is what Nietzsche writes, celebrating the comic poet: "I know of nothing that has caused me to dream more on Plato's secrecy and his sphinx nature than the happily preserved *petit fait* that under the pillow of his deathbed there was found no 'Bible,' nothing Egyptian, Pythagorean, or Platonic—but a volume of Aristophanes. How could even a Plato have endured life—a Greek life to which he said No—without an Aristophanes?" (VI 2: 43).

As when, once more in *Beyond Good and Evil*, Nietzsche writes of Plato's nobility: "There is something in the morality of Plato that does not really belong to Plato but is merely encountered in his philosophy, one might say, in spite of Plato: namely, the Socratism for which he was really too noble" (VI 2: 113).

As when, alongside the stern condemnation pronounced against Plato in *The Twilight of the Idols* ("Plato is boring . . ., is so moralistic, so preexistently Christian" [VI 3: 149]), Nietzsche also writes of Plato: "He says with an innocence for which one must be a Greek, not a 'Christian,' that there would be no Platonic philosophy at all if there were not such beautiful youths in Athens." Nietzsche continues: "Philosophy after the fashion of Plato might rather be defined as an erotic contest, as a further development and an inwardizing of the ancient agonistic gymnastics and of its *presuppositions*. What finally grew out of this philosophic eroticism of Plato? A new art form of the Greek agon, dialectic" (VI 3: 120).

As when, in *The Gay Science*, Nietzsche writes of Plato's healthiness and of his overpowerful senses: "All philosophical idealism hitherto was something like an illness, unless it was, as in the case of Plato, the caution of an over-rich and dangerous healthiness, the fear of *overpowerful* sense, the prudence of a prudent Socrates.—Perhaps we moderns are merely not healthy enough *to be in need of* Plato's idealism?" (V 2: 306).

As when, finally, in a notebook entry from the mid-1880s, Nietzsche writes of the inversion once effected by Plato, by Plato *the artist*, Plato *still* the artist: "Basically, Plato, as the artist he was, preferred appearance [*Schein*] to being: thus lie and invention to truth, the unreal to the actual. But he was so convinced of the value of appearance that he gave it the attributes 'being,' 'causality,' and 'goodness,' and 'truth,' in short everything men value" (VIII 1: 261).

It is remarkable how this image of Platonic inversion places even the origination of metaphysics more in the hands of Plato the artist than of Plato the Socratic moralist. It is the artist who set up that "true world" that was finally to become a fable, who set it up, however, precisely as appearance, as a fable, which it no doubt would have remained, had not the Socratic moralist inverted—or confused—the names *appearance* and *being*.

At the limit this figure of Nietzsche's Platonism begins, then, to communicate with, in a sense even to merge with, the first figure, the inverted Platonism of Nietzsche's own thought, which—like Plato the artist—would give preference to appearance over being, or at least to what, determined in opposition to being, had always been called appearance.

This is why to the very end Nietzsche remained a Greek, or rather sought, as from the beginning, to come back to the Greeks, as he declares with incomparable brilliance in the final paragraph of the last work he completed in his final creative year. Beyond these words written for the 1886 Preface to *The Gay Science* and then, finally, repeated at the end of *Nietzsche Contra Wagner*—beyond these words there is little more than silence: "Oh, those Greeks! They understood how to live. What is required for that is to remain courageously at the surface, the fold, the skin, to adore appearance [*Schein*], to believe in forms, tones, words, in the whole *Olympus of appearance*. Those Greeks were superficial—*out of profundity*. And is not this precisely what we are again coming back to, we daredevils of the spirit who have climbed the highest and most dangerous peak of present thought and looked around from up there—we who have *looked down* from there? Are we not, precisely in this respect, Greeks? Adorers of forms, of tones, of words? And therefore—artists?" (V 2: 20, repeated in VI 3: 437).

CHAPTER 2

THE POLITICS OF THE χώρα

IT BELONGS TO THE EXEMPLARY role accorded the Greeks in Arendt's work that she discovers in their political institutions and thought not only certain essential moments of political life that have subsequently been obscured but also the very operations that first obscured such moments and drove them to the margin of Western political thought. One such moment is action (πρᾶξις), which, according to Arendt's interpretation, Plato's thought submits to a fateful substitution. The substitution involves both a reduction and a subordination of action. It is a matter, first of all, of distinguishing knowledge from action in a way that gives knowledge primacy over action, substituting for knowledge operative within action a knowledge that would precede action and determine it in advance. This shift is, in turn, supported by a referral of political action to the paradigm of making (ποίησις), in which a certain knowledge, a vision of what is to be made, always precedes the actual fabrication. Making is, then, in effect substituted for action—that is, action is reduced to a subordinate phase within making. It is the paradigm of making—that is, of the orientation to a paradigm to be held in view in such a way that one might fabricate a product that looks like the paradigm—that comes to determine the orientation of subsequent political thought. This paradigm of the paradigm becomes all-decisive.

Arendt points to two effects of this orientation to making: first, it renders political thought essentially utopian, directed primarily to the vision and elaboration of the paradigm; second, it produces a degradation of politics into a means by which to achieve a higher end, namely, the making or remaking of the πόλις in the image of the paradigm. Arendt draws special attention to the way in which such a portrayal of the realm of human affairs as a sphere of making can acquire a connection with violence: within such a purview violence can come to be legitimated or even glorified as the necessary means for remaking the πόλις or the state. Thus she recalls Marx's dictum that "violence is the midwife of every old society pregnant with a new one."[1]

No doubt Arendt is correct in tracing such effects back to Plato's thought and, specifically, to the prominent role that making (ποίησις) plays in that thought. And yet, when one returns to the Platonic texts with these effects in mind, one cannot but be surprised at how openly those texts also go about limiting the hegemony of ποίησις. For example, in Book 10 of the *Republic* one finds a discussion in which Socrates introduces a certain differentiation: for each thing there are, he says, three τέχναι, one that will use the thing, one that will make it, and one that will imitate it. Socrates insists also on a hierarchical ordering of these τέχναι and, in particular, on the superiority of using over making: "It is quite necessary, then, that the man who uses each thing be most experienced and that he report to the maker what are the good or bad points, in actual use, of the instrument he uses. For example, about flutes, a flute player surely reports to the flute-maker which ones would serve him in playing, and he will prescribe how they must be made, and the other will serve him" (601d–e). Making is thus determined, limited, by a certain knowledge that can only come to it from outside its own sphere; it submits to a vision that only the user, not the maker himself, can provide. In most instances, of course, the using is itself, in turn, a kind of making: the flute player, who instructs the flute-maker about how the flute is to be made, uses the flute in order, in turn, to produce music, to make beautiful sounds. Nonetheless, the knowledge that the flute player provides to the maker is not the same as that operative in his own production of beautiful sounds, even though he will indeed have learned through the practice of his music-making how flutes ought to be made. The structure of making thus undergoes considerable complication: not only is it limited from above, receiving from the user its vision of the paradigm,

1. Hannah Arendt, *The Human Condition* (Garden City, N.Y.: Doubleday, 1959), 204.

but also within making as such there is a doubling of the operative forms of knowledge. Each artisan (τεχνίτης) is both maker and user, that is, he uses something in such a way as to make something else, as the flute player uses the flute to make music. But then he must both possess—have received, say, from the director—the knowledge of what is to be made, of what songs are to be played, and also have acquired through the practice of his τέχνη the vision to be communicated to the artisan below him in the hierarchy, the knowledge, for instance, of how the flute is to be made (in what form, with what capacities, etc.).

Yet, it is not only through the analysis of the order connecting different τέχναι that the Platonic text exposes an operation that limits ποίησις. Nor is it a matter only of extending the hierarchies of τέχναι up to their point of convergence in the statesman so as to reopen at that level the question of πρᾶξις, to reopen it by considering whether the statesman's action could ever be reappropriated once and for all to the sphere of ποίηοις and statecraft submitted, without remainder, to a philosophical vision of the good. It is not only from within and from above that the Platonic text shows ποίησις to be subject to the operation of limits but also, indeed most powerfully and intractably, from below. It is not only the freedom of action and use that interrupts and limits ποίησις but also, indeed first of all, a force of necessity to which ποίησις will always already have been submitted. The necessity is not that of a ruling paradigm and its law, but rather a necessity opposed to τέχνη and hence more like chance. It can be called the errant kind of cause, *errant* in various senses ranging from *wandering* to *straying* to *going astray*, to *erring*—the word thus itself wandering from sense to sense, its semantics enacting what, in a certain sense, it says. Within a certain kind of discourse called εἰκὼς λόγος (likely discourse in the sense of discourse on likenesses, discourse about images), this errant necessity is called *mother*, *nurse*, *receptacle*. But in the discourse that calls it by its proper—or at least most nearly proper—name, it is called χώρα. That discourse—Plato's chorology—occurs near the center of the *Timaeus*. Within this dialogue the chorology follows two other discourses: the initial discourse in which Socrates and then, in a very different fashion, Critias speak of politics, Socrates recapitulating the discussion on the previous day, Critias anticipating a political discourse to come; then, secondly, Timaeus' long discourse—actually the first of three—on the making (ποίησις) of the cosmos. The chorology is thus framed—indeed on both sides—by discourses on ποίησις and on politics.

The antecedent discourses carry out, not—as it might seem—an unlimited affirmation of ποίησις, but an interrogation and marking of its limits. This at any rate is what is to be shown. It will be shown also that the chorology gathers the limits disclosed in the antecedent discourses. Saying the χώρα proves to be a way—indeed the most originary way—of saying the limits of ποίησις, and hence of declaring the limits that both govern and threaten any political discourse oriented to ποίησις. In saying these limits, the chorology and the *Timaeus* at large broach a politics of the χώρα.

Yet what about the appearance of unlimited affirmation, the semblance that the history of Western thought has almost continuously translated into reality, into an allegedly Platonic origin of utopian political thought? What about Arendt's account of this history? If the Platonic texts indeed pose the limits of ποίησις, limits from within, from above, and especially from below, how can Plato's thought have had the effect described so accurately and convincingly in Arendt's discussions? How is it that ποίησις can have determined *without limit* the basic orientation of political thought in the lineage of Plato's *Republic?*

The utopian effect of the Platonic texts was a determined result, determined by a certain way of reading those texts, which is to say also a way of *not* reading, of refusing to read. The way of reading and not reading that produced the utopian effect was itself, in turn, determined by an orientation to a certain restricted economy, that is, by a demand that everything exposed by the reading be situated within that economy, appropriated to it. Even such submission to an economy may be considered to have its Platonic precedent, at least if one grants with Arendt that Platonic thought extends the law of the household to the regulation of the πόλις at large.[2] But what is decisive in the economy that comes to regulate the history of the reading and nonreading of the Platonic texts is the reduction of the χώρα that it enforces. By reducing the χώρα, by excluding its power to limit ποίησις and to disrupt every unlimited affirmation of ποίησις, the operation of the economy serves to preclude the commencement of a politics of the χώρα.

2. Ibid., 199f.

The history of the reading and nonreading of the *Timaeus* mirrors within this single dimension many of the motifs and operations at work in the history of metaphysics at large, most notably, the operation of an economy of meaning that has the effect of domesticating the χώρα. This correspondence results from the prevalence of the *Timaeus* in the development of the history of metaphysics. For there is no text in the Western philosophical tradition that has been more continuously read or that has been more interwoven in the fabric of Western metaphysics. The *Timaeus* was the subject of debate among Plato's early successors in the Academy and, of course, for Aristotle. It was a subject of commentary by Plutarch, Plotinus, and Proclus, and it was widely known during the Middle Ages in the Latin translation by Chalcidius; it was indeed the primary genuinely Platonic source of medieval Platonism. It remained effective throughout much of the modern period. It proved especially significant for the German Idealists; the recent publication of Schelling's early manuscripts on the *Timaeus* has served to confirm that the dialogue played a decisive role in the formation of Schelling's early thought.[3]

Suffice it here merely to mark a single passage from Aristotle and its remote echo in Hegel. The passage from Aristotle, discussed in detail and in larger context in *Chorology*,[4] appears to constitute one of the primary points of inception of the metaphysical economy, at least as regards the reduction of the χώρα. The passage occurs in Book 4 of the *Physics*. It is a remarkable blend of reading and nonreading: "This is why Plato says in the *Timaeus* that matter and the χώρα are the same; for the receptive and the χώρα are one and the same. Although the manner in which he speaks about the receptive in the *Timaeus* differs from that in the so-called unwritten teachings, nevertheless he declares that place and the χώρα are the same" (209b).

The passage is remarkable for its lack of correspondence with the text of the *Timaeus*. It poses three identifications: that the receptive (μεταληπτικόν) and the χώρα are the same; that matter (ὕλη)

3. F. W. J. Schelling, "*Timaeus*." *(1794)*, ed. Hartmut Buchner (Stuttgart-Bad Cannstatt: Frommann-Holzboog, 1994). Additional material belonging to Schelling's early Plato studies appears as two appendices in Michael Franz, *Schellings Tübinger Platon-Studien* (Göttingen: Vanderhoeck and Ruprecht, 1996). See my discussion of these texts in *Chorology*, 155–67.

4. *Chorology*, 151–54. For translation and interpretation of the chorology, see 113–24.

and the χώρα are the same; and that place (τόπος) and the χώρα are the same. Of these three identifications, only the first has any justification in the text of the *Timaeus* and then only if one erases any difference that might be connoted between μεταληπτικόν and the Platonic words δεχόμενον and ὑποδοχή. For the identification of the χώρα with matter (ὕλη) there is little textual warrant and certainly none that could justify a simple, straightforward identification: for though one of the images presented of the χώρα is that of the gold on which all figures may be impressed but which itself is none of these figures and can be none of them if it is to be equally receptive of all, this is only one image among several, to say nothing of the fact that it is an *image of* the χώρα, not an identification of it as such. One cannot but suspect that the identification posed by Aristotle serves precisely to transpose into the economy of Aristotle's thought a moment of the Platonic discourse that would otherwise either simply escape or else disrupt that economy.

The third identification is less obviously unjustified: one can indeed find numerous passages in the dialogues where χώρα is used in a sense closely allied to that of τόπος, and it is not surprising that English translators of the *Timaeus*, from Thomas Taylor on, have most often rendered χώρα as *place*. The difficulty here is that the chorology—the scant half-page near the center of the *Timaeus* (52a–d)—insists on the differentiation between χώρα and τόπος. Speaking of the χώρα as itself withdrawing from speech, touching upon it as to be touched without sense and only by a sort of bastard reckoning, Timaeus says: "and looking toward which we dream and affirm that it is necessary that all that is be somewhere in some place [τόπος] and occupy some χώρα" (52b). Whatever identification of χώρα and τόπος this passage may suggest is vigorously retracted as Timaeus continues: "Under the influence of this dreaming, we are unable to awaken, to distinguish [these], and to say the truth. . . ." In the dream, then, we conflate precisely what it is necessary in truth to differentiate; it is only in the dream that we identify χώρα and τόπος and believe that to think the χώρα is simply to affirm that everything that is is somewhere, in some place. The Aristotelian text too remains absorbed in this dream, appropriating the χώρα to τόπος, dreaming of a place of all places that also has a place within the economy of the *Physics*, offering only the slightest hint that the χώρα might be addressed somewhat differently in the unwritten teachings.

Hegel, too, translates χώρα into place, the place (*Ort*) in which things are produced. Hegel uses the word *erzeugt—produced, fabricated,* but also *procreated, begotten*—thus reinscribing in his text an oscillation that runs throughout the *Timaeus* and that reflects at the level of semantics one of the primary ways in which the dialogue brings ποίησις into question. Nonetheless, Hegel essentially repeats the Aristotelian reduction of the χώρα, translating it into *place* and even identifying it with "passive matter."[5] Little wonder that in reading the *Timaeus* Hegel can so easily recognize there what his *Logic* calls the concept, the idea—most notably in the world-soul's gathering of the cosmos into a whole.[6]

The enforcement of the reduction of the χώρα, the forcing of it into the economy of meaning, which metaphysics—as a certain Platonism—will put in force, is thus carried out especially in and through translation, for example in Chalcidius' translation of it as *locus* and in Thomas Taylor's rendering of it as *place*. What is decisive is that translating χώρα—either within Greek or from Greek to another language—functions also as a way of saying what χώρα means. It serves as an instrument by which to forge, even if indirectly, a connection of the χώρα to a meaning, that is, to an intelligible εἶδος. To translate χώρα, for instance, as *place*, is to say that both words have the same semantic correlate, the same meaning, translation consisting in the move from one word to the other by way of the common meaning. To grant the possibility of translation is, then, to grant the legitimacy of bringing an eidetic determination to bear on the χώρα. But the χώρα, says Timaeus, is a third kind, distinct from the intelligible εἴδη and equally distinct from those things that are sensible and generated and that, sharing both name and looks with the intelligible, are subject to eidetic determination, that is, have meaning. The χώρα has no meaning, and to translate it, to submit it to eidetic determination, is to appropriate it to an economy of meaning, to violate it. Can it be that the entire history of the reading of the *Timaeus* has been haunted by this specter of violence?

---

5. G. W. F. Hegel, *Vorlesungen über die Geschichte der Philosophie* II, in *Werke* (Frankfurt a.M.: Suhrkamp, 1971), 19: 100f.

6. Ibid., 93.

In order to show how the *Timaeus* broaches a politics of the χώρα, one must reread outside all eidetic economy not only the chorology but also the other discourses insofar as they serve to expose the limits that are then gathered into the χώρα. Yet as one turns to begin rereading the dialogue, one will soon be overtaken by the question: Where is one to begin? Presumably at the beginning—following the injunction given in the *Timaeus*, though not at the beginning, the injunction: "With regard to everything it is most important to begin at the natural beginning" (29b). But where is the natural beginning? What is the natural beginning? Could one not say that the χώρα is the natural beginning, that is, the beginning of nature, the mother from whom nature is born? The question of beginning thus leads directly into the thick of the questioning that the dialogue unfolds. Here already there is an indication of how thoroughly the question of beginning is pursued in the *Timaeus*.

If nonetheless one adheres to the apparent linearity of the text and begins rereading at or near the point where the text begins, one's assurance of having begun at the beginning will not for long be sustained: for in the opening remarks by Socrates and the very brief discussion that follows upon them, what seems to be a beginning is collapsed by a reference back to another beginning, the discussion on the previous day, which is to be continued in the present discussion. For purposes of that continuation Socrates complies with Timaeus' request that he recount that previous discussion, that other beginning, that he recount it from the beginning (ἐξ ἀρχῆς). This palintropic structure, that of a beginning collapsed as such by reference back to a prior beginning, is one that recurs in virtually every dimension of the *Timaeus*. It is, most notably, the structure by which the discourse comes to open upon the χώρα.

Socrates begins: "The chief part of the discourse I delivered yesterday was about the constitution [πολιτεία], what sort seemed to me best and from what sort of men it came" (17c). The discourse preceding the beginning of the *Timaeus* and now to be recounted is thus a discourse on the πολιτεία, a discussion of the constitution of the πόλις, a discourse on the political ordering of—to translate, cautiously, with reservations—the city. At least, this political discourse constitutes the chief part of the discourse delivered on the previous day. One should note that the word translated as *the chief part* (τὸ κεφάλαιον) means literally: what belongs to the head (κεφαλή). In this regard one should recall the name of a character who speaks very near the beginning of the dialogue actually entitled πολιτεία (translated *Res publica, Republic*): Cephalus was nothing but head, an old man who had lost all the desires of the body, one on the threshold of death. Especially if a discourse is supposed to have all the parts corresponding to those of a living being—to recall the well-known injunction from the *Phaedrus* (264c)—then one cannot but wonder about the discourse that Socrates is now to recount, since it is *only the head* of the discourse delivered on the previous day. One cannot entirely suppress one's suspicion about the recapitulation with which Socrates begins, which is also a kind of inverse decapitation that leaves out of account, that refuses to recount, the rest of the discursive body.

Recounting the head of the discourse, Socrates speaks of the ordering of the city, its ordering according to τέχνη, according to ποίησις carried out through the practice of the various τέχναι.[7] As a site for the practice of τέχνη, it is essentially a *technical city*. Each citizen is to practice only his or her own τέχνη, the one to which he or she is best suited by nature. The best πολιτεία, the best ordering of the city, will be the one according to which each does what is proper to him or her. Socrates stresses that such propriety is especially imperative for those who are to defend the city. It is thus that they are to have everything in common, to have no private property, the pursuit of which would otherwise distract them from devotion to excellence in their one τέχνη, drawing them, for instance, into another, a money-making τέχνη that could not but impair their capacity to defend the city. In this best of cities, in order that it be the best of cities, there is to be no regard paid to sexual difference: women are also to be assigned their one sole τέχνη, and even those who become guardians are to be treated no differently from the men. Socrates then mentions procreation and, calling attention to the novelty of this proposal, declares that in this regard, too, all are to have all in common. Each should recognize all as his kinsmen, as brothers and sisters, as parents and grandparents, or as children and grandchildren, depending on age. The actual production of children is to be controlled so as to produce the best offspring; this will require that the rulers

---

7. On the sense of τέχνη and its relation to ποίησις, see *Chorology*, 15–17.

contrive means to control mating so that good mate with good and bad with bad.

One should note the word that Socrates uses in introducing these novel proposals regarding procreation: he says παιδοποιία, literally child-production, child-making, as though procreation were a matter of ποίησις, of fabricating one's offspring. Indeed, the ordering of the relations between the guardians is such that what results is a kind of fabricated community. Where the fabrication fails to control fully the product, when, for instance, having contrived that the bad mate with the bad, having sent their offspring off to some other part of the city outside the citadel of the guardians, when it then turns out that, despite all that the τέχνη of child-production can do, some such offspring prove worthy, then those who are worthy must be recalled to the citadel and their opposites, the children of the good who have proved undeserving, must be put in their place outside. It is precisely in Socrates' reference to this place outside to which the undeserving will be sent that the word χώρα occurs for the first time in the *Timaeus*. From the outset it is posed at the margin of what can be fabricated, marking the limit of ποίησις.

The community to be fabricated among the guardians, all having all in common, is to supplement the natural community, the familial community. The fabricated community is to compensate for the ills of the natural community and thus to constitute the citadel around which the best of cities will be built. In compensating for those ills, the supplementary, fabricated community will also tend to replace and displace the natural community, indeed so thoroughly that it will even come to be taken as the natural community, each thus regarding all as his actual kinsmen. The most telling index of this supplemental replacement and displacement of nature is its inevitably introducing into the community something utterly contrary to nature, namely, incest. According to the fabricated kinship system, one will inevitably mate with one's kin, indeed in every case, since each is the kin of all; all mating will be tainted by incest. Furthermore, since the fabricated kinship system is to displace and thus efface natural kinship, Socrates remarking explicitly that one is never to recognize one's own offspring, one can—and no doubt some will—happen to mate with a natural kinsman. And if the fabricated system is sufficiently effective in its work of effacement, one can—and no doubt some will—happen to mate with kin without the slightest knowledge that one is doing so.[8] The result is a community fabricated in the image of Oedipus, the best of cities transformed into a scene of tragedy.

Yet it is not so much as a scene of tragedy that this city is inscribed in the Platonic texts but rather as a subject of comedy.[9] The technical city is to be so rigorously ordered by τέχνη that even mating and procreation would be brought under control, as though these were only matters of the head, as though ἔρως could be brought under technical control and its disruptive power dissolved or at least marginalized, transferred to that place outside to which those are sent who, despite being offspring of the good, turn out to be undeserving. In this capital city the eruption of ἔρως across the field of sexual difference would be submitted to technical control and sexual difference effectively effaced along with the natural family. The entire city would be brought under the order of ποίησις and made into a self-enclosed unity in which all needs would be supplied by the organization of the τέχναι. At its center, in the citadel of the guardians who would protect it from any encroachments from outside, the rule of the order of ποίησις would be unlimited.

But it is a matter of inverse decapitation, of a capital city that would be cut off from the erotic necessities of the body. As in a little comedy that breaks out in the course of Timaeus' long discourse on the making of the cosmos: the comedy depicts the prospect of the human head rolling along on the earth, coming upon heights and hollows of all sorts, and being at a loss as to how to climb over the heights and out of the hollows; thus it was, declares Timaeus, that a body was attached to the head as its vehicle of transportation (44d–e).

There is a proliferation of such comedy in the *Republic*. Though it is highly debatable whether, as Proclus thought,[10] the dramatic dates of the *Republic* and the *Timaeus* are such that the *Republic* can simply be identified with that discourse of the previous day that Socrates recapitulates in the *Timaeus*, it is manifest that the account given in

8. On the question of incest in the *Republic* and the *Timaeus*, see ibid., 20–21.

9. The comedy of the city is treated in greater detail and with more consideration of context in *Chorology*, 24–31, and in *Being and Logos: Reading the Platonic Dialogues*, 3rd ed. (Bloomington: Indiana University Press, 1996), 371–78.

10. See Proclus, *In Platonis Timaeum Commentaria*, ed. E. Diehl (Amsterdam: Verlag Adolf M. Hakkert, 1965), 1: 26. See *Chorology*, 21–23.

the *Timaeus* corresponds very closely to that building of the city in discourse that is carried out in Books 2–5 of the *Republic*—in other words, that in both dialogues it is the same city that is being fabricated in λόγος. In the *Republic* that discursive fabrication culminates in an extended comedy that is literally played out by Socrates and Glaucon: imagining the sight of women exercising naked with the men in the palaestras, Socrates refers to the jokes that would be made if gymnastic practices were so altered as to permit such sights; he speaks even of comedies regarding such things. He goes on to lay down a kind of mock standard for comedy: "He is empty who . . . tries to produce laughter looking to any sight as ridiculous other than the sight of the foolish and the bad" (452d). Then Socrates and Glaucon conspicuously open the performance by way of a pretended conversation with those who disagree with them. Once the dialogue is thus folded back upon itself, the comedy gives voice to the outrageous demand for "a community of pleasure and pain" (462b). This demand presupposes a total disregard for the utter singularity of the body and of the pleasures and pains bound to it, and the comedy, one realizes, is only playing out a disregard for something that can in deed never be disregarded. Sexual difference also enters into the play: the difference between men and women is—comically—reduced to something analogous to the difference between bald and long-haired men (454c). What is at issue is perhaps most succinctly expressed when, in response to Socrates' description of the prescribed mating practices, Glaucon insists on the difference between, as he says, geometrical necessities and erotic necessities. In all its extravagant disregard the comedy of the city serves to disclose the incapacity of the city—of this fabricated, capital, inversely decapitated city—to incorporate ἔρως and all that is linked to the erotic, that is, mating, procreation, birth, sexual difference, corporeity itself in its singularity. By playing out this extravagant disregard for the erotic, the comedy exposes the disregard precisely as comic. What is marked by the comedy and by the recounting of it in the *Timaeus* is the limit of ποίησις with respect to ἔρως.

As Socrates turns from recounting the discourse of yesterday to proposing what he would now like to hear in exchange, his language becomes highly erotic: he speaks of seeing beautiful living beings and being moved by the desire to behold them in motion. His proposal is, then, for a discourse that would depict the city in motion, that is, at war. One cannot help asking why beholding the city in motion means observing it in war. Why could it not be in motion without going to war? Why could it not be in motion simply by having all the arts properly ordered and actually being practiced within the city? At least one reason is that there is one art that can be practiced only in war, namely, that of the guardians. This is to say, then, that the city cannot remain simply a self-enclosed, ordered totality of artisans, that the technical closure of the city will never succeed. The city will always also be related to an outside, an other.

In this regard one should recall that in the *Republic* the only city that is a self-enclosed community of artisans is the first in that series of cities fabricated in λόγος, the simple city of artisans, each practicing his τέχνη in harmony with the others, the city that the erotic Glaucon calls a "city of sows" (372d). On the other hand, as soon as the so-called unnecessary desires come into play, the city can no longer be simply unto itself; it cannot remain self-enclosed, self-sufficient. For in order to satisfy the additional desires, it has to expand, to take some land, some material resources, from another city and so go to war. As Socrates expresses it, anticipating the developments released in the *Timaeus*, the χώρα (here the word means, most immediately, *territory* or *land*) that was previously sufficient for the needs of the city now proves too small, and it becomes necessary to take some of the χώρα of neighboring cities (373d). This transition, one that presumably every city will in deed always already have made, points up the dependence of ποίησις on resources that it does not produce, its dependence on materials that lie outside the order of ποίησις.

In this regard one should also recall how the comedy of the city is briefly resumed at the end of Book 7 of the *Republic*. Likened by Glaucon to a sculptor producing fair men—and women, Socrates adds—Socrates proposes finally that the founding of the new city will require that everyone who is more than ten years of age be driven out (540e–541a). In order that the ruler-sculptor be able to shape the city in the image of the paradigm, it must first be transformed into a city of children, who like the marble used by the sculptor are still sufficiently unformed and can provide the necessary human material for the political ποίησις. Casting the child-citizens as raw material, like metals mined from the earth (as in the noble lie the rulers will enforce), the comedy serves to show that there are limits to political ποίησις, that a city of human citizens does not submit without limits to being remade in the image of some utopian paradigm.

Socrates' discourse on the city, even simply as recounted, has the effect of marking three kinds of limits that bear upon political ποίησις: its limitation by ἔρως and all that is linked to the erotic; its limitation by the relation to an outside, to other cities; and its limitation by its dependence on material. Yet, it is not only in the opening discourse that such limits are exposed but also in virtually every discursive phase and level of the *Timaeus*, though of course in various connections and in ways determined by the topology of the dialogue as a whole.

For example, in Timaeus' extended first discourse (the first of three), he tells how the god made the cosmos. The god he calls a δημιουργός (28a), that is, an artisan or craftsman, someone who makes things by practicing a τέχνη, like those artisans by each of whom a single τέχνη is to be practiced, at least according to the prescriptions expressed in the *Republic* and repeated in Socrates' recounting at the beginning of the *Timaeus*. Near the outset of the discourse on the cosmos Timaeus also calls the god τεκταινόμενος (28c); he is a technician, a builder, a maker. It is hardly surprising, then, that Timaeus describes the schema of the god's making of the cosmos in a way that submits it quite precisely to the structure of ποίησις: in producing something an artisan looks to the paradigm and crafts the product according to the model, makes the thing in such a way as to make it look like the paradigm. Likewise with the divine artisan: he looks to the intelligible paradigm and makes the cosmos look like it, makes the cosmos in the image, into an image, of the paradigm.

This orientation to ποίησις remains in force throughout the entire discourse. And yet, the discourse does not simply submit to this orientation but also marks certain points at which the limits of this schema come to light. Three such points may be mentioned.

The first comes in Timaeus' account of how the body of the cosmos was made. In this production, Timaeus says, the god used up all the elements, so that nothing was left over from which another cosmos could be made. Thus it was assured that there would be only one cosmos, that the cosmos would be one. Furthermore, by thus leaving nothing outside, the god made the body of the cosmos immune to aging and to illness, which always come upon a body, says Timaeus, "from outside." Though he leaves it unsaid, it follows that the body would also be relieved of the possibility of death. Timaeus says too that the god made the body of the cosmos in the shape of a sphere, because a sphere is similar to itself, self-same, each point equidistant from the center. Thus it was made in the image of intelligible, i.e., utterly selfsame, being. Timaeus continues, saying that the body of the cosmos was made smooth all around. Since there was nothing outside it to see or hear, it had no need of those openings to the outside that are called eyes and ears. Since there was no air surrounding it, it had no need of an organ of respiration by which otherwise air would be exchanged between inside and outside. It needed no hands either for grasping or for repelling someone, as in that violent clash with the other that erupts as war. Neither did it need feet with which to venture forth somewhere, to another place. On the contrary, shaping it into a perfectly smooth, uniform surface, the god spun it around uniformly in the same spot. Thus, the body of the cosmos was made self-sufficient, indeed so much so that, as Timaeus says, broaching a bit of comedy: "Nothing went out from it or came into it from anywhere, since there was nothing; it was designed to feed itself on its own waste and to act and be acted upon by itself and within itself" (33c–d). Thus, the body of the cosmos proves to be so thoroughly self-enclosed that it nourishes itself on its own excrement and affects, feels, only itself. In other words, it is the cosmic analogue of the city of artisans, completely self-enclosed, self-sufficient, lacking all relation to the outside, to an other. The little comedy serves to expose the very limit that has been comically disregarded, the limit constituted by the relation to the outside, to the other.

The second point lies in the very way the discourse sets out its project, in its oscillation between the language of making, of fabrication, and that of procreation, of begetting. For example, the δημιουργός is called both the maker (ποιητής) and the father (πατήρ) of the cosmos. And, perhaps most obtrusively, the cosmos, this product of divine ποίησις, is characterized as a living being made in the image of the paradigm of living being—as if Timaeus had forgotten that living beings are, most certainly, begotten and born, not made. Yet, this forgetfulness is only a comic enactment serving to mark the irrepressible reference of the order of ποίησις to that of procreation and birth.

The third point occurs in the transition from Timaeus' first discourse to his subsequent discourse, and the limit marked here is what necessitates this transition. Though it goes unmentioned within the first discourse, what comes to be noted in the transition is that the god, in setting out to make the cosmos, simply uses the four elements that are somehow already there. These elements have to be brought to the order of ποίησις from outside that order. It is precisely this reference back to a precosmic origin that marks again a limit of ποίησις and that, at this point in the dialogue, necessitates the new beginning, the turn back to this beginning before the beginning, the turn that soon leads to the chorology.

In the chorology and the prelude to it, the limits of ποίησις exposed in the preceding discourses are gathered up and thought together in the χώρα. This third kind grants an abode (ἕδρα) to things of the second kind, things that come to be; it lets these phantoms, as Timaeus says, cling "to being at least in a certain way, on pain of being nothing at all" (52c); it lets them be outside the first kind, outside the sphere of the intelligible εἴδη, yet still cling to being, still avoid being nothing at all. One could say—though not without some risk of falling into the dream in which the χώρα is conflated with place—that the χώρα is the other of being, not just in the sense of being other (ἕτερον) than being (as every εἶδος except being would be other than being), but rather in a more abysmal sense, in a sense irreducible to a difference of sense. One could say, too, that the χώρα is the outside of being, that it is what enables externality as such and thus makes it possible for something outside being nonetheless to be. One could say of the χώρα that its capacity to disperse being is set over against the gathering power of being itself. Furthermore, as the discourses immediately surrounding the chorology declare, the χώρα is precisely the outside from which arises the material that must be taken over by the order of ποίησις. The χώρα is a receptacle filled in the beginning with indeterminate powers in flux; it is the mother from whom, then, the elements come to be born. And as mother and receptacle, the χώρα is outside the productive order; it is allied with birth, procreation, and all that is linked to ἔρως. Or rather, it is the outside of the productive order, that which limits ποίησις; it is a third kind that limits and yet also makes possible that circulation between the other two kinds that is called ποίησις.

The chorology would provide, then, a way of thinking the difference between a city built in λόγος and an actual city formed in the image of the paradigm. It would be a matter of thinking this difference, not merely as a gap between fact and ideal that could be gradually narrowed by political means, by employing politics as a productive means, or, as Arendt would say, degrading it into a means; to think this difference by way of the χώρα would be, rather, to think it as displacement to the outside of being, just as, according to the chorology sensible things come to be outside of being, even if sharing both name and looks with being. Or rather, one would need to think this difference as inaugural emplacement outside being, in the outside of being, as submission to the dispersal that holds apart from being. It is as if there were in the opposite direction an exceeding of being comparable to that granted to the good as ἐπέκεινα τῆς οὐσίας. The actual city, set in place on the earth, would differ from the paradigm in a sense irreducible to a difference of sense. Such are, in any case, some of the things that can be said about this difference, as, falling also back into the dream, one struggles to remain wakeful.

Such a thinking of difference, of displacement, would broach a politics of the χώρα. Is such a politics to be found in the Platonic texts? In the *Laws* perhaps? One cannot but be struck by the very frequent occurrence of the word χώρα in the *Laws*, its occurrence with incomparably greater frequency than in any other dialogue (including the *Timaeus*); and yet, for the most part the word seems to have settled back into its prephilosophical senses (land, territory, country) rather than calling forth the level of the discourse woven around the word in the chorology. But whether, in any case, the turn that the *Laws* takes to the second-best πολιτεία (739e), along with its insistence on a blending of monarchy and democracy—which the Athenian calls the two mothers of all constitutions (693d, cf. 756e)—whether these moves draw the lines of a politics of the χώρα is a question that could be answered only by a more patient and careful reading of this vast text than can be undertaken here. It must suffice to have raised the question.

But what of a politics of the χώρα today? If the bearing of thinking today is to be taken from Nietzsche's inversion and exhaustion of Platonism, from his twisting free of the founding distinction of Platonism, then the requirements for thinking the politics of the χώρα will be rigorously determined. Everything will depend on thinking the outside of being otherwise than in opposition to the absolute interiority of selfsame being, of the intelligible εἶδος. One will need to think beings as taking place without thinking them as images secured in their being, in their identity, by their imaging of absolutely secure, self-identical beings. One will need in this sense to think beings without being; or, again in this sense, to think them not as beings.

Now they will need to be thought as taking place in a place in which all the markers of security and certainty would have disappeared, in a place that, like the city itself, would be irreducible to place, a place that would also not be a place, a place that would not settle into place. Could one, then, begin to rethink the πολιτεία in reference to place in this sense (a sense that is irreducible to sense)? Could one begin to rethink the constitution of the city or the state as withdrawn from the rule of any paradigmatic ἀρχή, as withdrawn from the monarch or government that, possessing power, would enforce the paradigm represented? Could one think it, instead, as a place not to be possessed, appropriated, and in that sense occupied, an empty place, as, for example, in Lefort's schema of democracy in which the exercise of power is subject to the procedures of periodic redistribution, so that those who exercise power do not thereby possess power, appropriate it to themselves, like a monarch? Or a dictator?[11]

And yet, would one not need to think the constitution of the political not only as a distinctive place but also as taking place in a distinctive way? Venturing to think dispersal not just as holding apart from being but as dispersal without being, a politics of the χώρα would think political constitution as taking place both on the earth in its elemental bearing and also in a cosmos that can neither provide a point of security nor itself be secured by reference to a paradigm or center or origin. Whatever is politically constituted takes place in an unsurveyable cosmos running endlessly from nowhere to nowhere. Still, as in the *Timaeus*, political discourse would be inseparable from cosmological discourse.

In any case, a politics of the χώρα will never be a simple linear discourse, one that could be confident of having begun at the beginning, one that could with assurance dispense with all need to double back upon itself, taking back what it has said, even while granting that it will not be able to forgo saying such things again, falling back into the dream. But one thing is certain: a politics of the χώρα will never provide a prescription for making or remaking the πόλις; it will

11. See Claude Lefort, *Democracy and Political Theory*, trans. David Macey (Minneapolis: University of Minnesota Press, 1988), especially 17–19.

never issue in a paradigm in reference to which that degraded politics of which Arendt writes would then set about fabricating the πόλις, looking to the paradigm so as to make the πόλις in its image. Rather, a politics of the χώρα would look instead to the limits of every such ποίησις and would undertake to think what comes into play at these limits.

In *The Life of the Mind* Arendt describes the quarrel between the ancients and the moderns in the following way: "The famous 'quarrel between the ancients and the moderns' actually turns on the question of what the aim of knowledge is; is it 'to save the phenomena,' as the ancients believed, or to discover the hidden functional apparatus which makes them appear?"[12] The accomplishment of Plato's *Timaeus* is that it settles this quarrel before it can even have begun. The *Timaeus* settles the quarrel by replacing its either/or with a both/and: especially in the chorology it both saves the phenomena and discovers what makes them appear. Yet the dialogue accomplishes this in a way that radically undercuts the traditional understanding of what it means to save the phenomena and to discover the hidden functional apparatus that makes them appear. In the *Timaeus* phenomena are saved by being thought in emplacement outside being, where, even though they share both name and looks with the intelligible, they are other than it; it is in their irrecoupable otherness that they are distinctively phenomenal, saved as phenomena from appropriation to the intelligible. At the same time, the chorology discloses the hidden apparatus—Timaeus calls the χώρα an invisible εἶδος—by which phenomena appear, by which they are granted the abode in which they can appear as phenomena, that is, as other than the intelligible, as other in a sense irreducible to intelligibility, irreducible to sense.

12. Hannah Arendt, *The Life of the Mind* (New York: Harcourt, Brace, Jovanovich, 1981), 1: 53.

CHAPTER 3

DAYDREAM

"—*der Traum ist ausgeträumt.*"

—E. Husserl

IT IS IMPERATIVE.

It is even the imperative of imperatives.

One is to begin—so says this imperative—by turning to the things themselves.

This is what is required in order that thinking be rigorous: that it proceed from things themselves, that it take its bearings solely from them, that it take entirely from them the truth that would be declared, itself contributing nothing except the detaching of that truth from the things themselves, its detachment in a form that can be declared, its transcription. It would be difficult to say what belongs to—and what delimits—philosophy that does not also lie within the arc of this turn. Or at the points from which and to which the arc swings. Or rather, in the intervals that open at these points, displacing them, erasing them. Once one has caught a glimpse of these openings, one can declare—reproducing, almost, the very opening in question—that the detachment of truth from the things themselves is not itself taken from the things themselves, that transcription cannot but transmute εἰς ἀλλὸ γένος. And turning back toward the beginning, one can declare also that the very turn to the things themselves opens an interval, a moment of near-blindness, an indeterminate space across which one's vision would first come to adhere to the things themselves—at least to the extent that, between this and the other interval, rigor is not merely a dream that one would finally have dreamed out. But this interval, that of the beginning and of the deferral of beginning, this interval in which, as Timaeus says, "we intend to make a suitable beginning [. . . μέλλομεν ἄρξεσθαι κατὰ τρόπον]" (*Tim.* 54a), the duplicity of the word (μέλλω) opening precisely this interval (to intend to begin, to be about to begin, is also to delay, to defer the very beginning that one is about to make)—this interval would surely be difficult to distinguish from a dream. Difficult—that is, χαλεπόν—hence also: troublesome, even dangerous.

This indicator, the word χαλεπόν, is one of the most decisive in the *Timaeus*, and its resonance ought not be lost as one turns back to the dream, returning to it, as near the end of a text by Jacques Derrida that bears—even in French—the English title "Tense": "Return to the dream, then, the dream that we never abandoned, for still 'we are imagining that we are dreaming.' We recall that Plato says of χώρα that we perceive it as in a dream (*Tim.* 52b–c)."[1] The self-citation refers to the opening words of "Tense": "Let us imagine. Let us imagine that we are dreaming."[2] Dreaming of what? Dreaming, in French, of inventing an *autre temps*. Derrida asks that the translator leave these two last words in their original language, and he leaves this request itself, set in parentheses, in the text of "Tense." This *autre temps* is to be a gift, invented and offered in the time of the dream. Unless—says Derrida—the recipient has already invented it himself: "Unless—and we are now in the time of the dream—unless he has already done it himself."[3] In this case the economy of the gift would

1. Jacques Derrida, "Tense," trans. D. F. Krell, in *The Path of Archaic Thinking: Unfolding the Work of John Sallis*, ed. Kenneth Maly (Albany: State University of New York Press, 1995), 73. The present text may be read as continuing a discussion that began with a brief presentation I gave at Cerisy-la-Salle in 1992. The presentation was oriented to Derrida's *Khôra* (Paris: Galilée, 1993), which appeared in the first version in *Poikilia: Études offertes à Jean-Pierre Vernant* (Paris: EHESS, 1987) and in an English translation by Ian McLeod in *On the Name* (Stanford: Stanford University Press, 1995). My presentation has appeared in French ("De la Chôra," in *Le passage des frontières: Autour du travail de Jacques Derrida* [Paris: Galilée, 1994]) and in English ("Of the Χώρα," *Epoché* II/1 (1994): 1–12). Derrida takes up and extends the discussion in "Tense," especially pp. 70–74, together with note 11 (p. 284), which refers to "De la Chôra."

2. Ibid., 49.

3. Ibid.

be interrupted or at least put in question: for how could one give time to someone who, through his own invention, already had time? And how could the recipient give something in turn, something of comparable value, which could only be, again, to give time? How—except by differentiation? And by insistence. By insisting that it be, always and even at the same time (*tout à la fois*, ἅμα), an *autre temps*.

A time as other, as marked by alterity. Such time as that of the dream of the χώρα. Or rather, what one would call such, were it not in every respect anterior to the operation of such structures as that of the *such*.

Let us begin by taking this time as that of the χώρα, as the time of which one would also dream in dreaming of the χώρα. Then it would be indeed an *autre temps*, a time other than time, a time before time, a time "before everything," as Derrida says, "the absolute antecedent."[4] It would be a time different even from the time of day, the time measured out by the course of the sun across the sky. Heidegger takes the day to be indeed "the 'most natural' measure of time."[5] But the time of the χώρα, this *autre temps*, is not measured by the day and by the course of the sun. It is a time anterior to such measure, a time anterior—it would seem—to all measure. There is (*il y a*) this unmeasured, measureless time before the sun comes to bring measure and illumination to all things. There is (*il y a*) this time before the day, before sunrise—a time that is not just night, not just the time after nightfall with its promise of the coming sunrise, but rather an *autre nuit*, "*l'autre nuit [qui] est toujours autre*."[6] A night that never becomes day, ever-prevailing darkness. Like Hades.

The time of the χώρα is not yet even a time of imagination. It is not a time in which one could imagine; one could not even imagine imagining in this time. Not, at least, if imagining is taken to consist in somehow bringing images to presence before, as we say, the mind's eye. For the time to which Timaeus' discourse on the χώρα is directed is a time before the generation of the heaven (πρὸ τῆς οὐρανοῦ γενέσεως [*Tim.* 48b; cf. 52d]). It is a time in which there are not yet

4. Derrida, "Avances," preceding: Serge Margel, *Le Tombeau du Dieu Artisan* (Paris: Les Éditions de Minuit, 1995), 12.

5. Martin Heidegger, *Sein und Zeit* (Tübingen: Max Niemeyer Verlag, 1960), 413.

6. Maurice Blanchot, *L'Espace Littéraire* (Paris: Gallimard, 1955), 222.

any images whatsoever, a time when—in the absence of the artisan god (53b), while he is, as it were, idle—even the simplest of things (of what will be transmuted into sensible images), fire, air, water, and earth, are *not yet themselves*, are not yet properly images but only *traces* of themselves as such (ἴχνη . . . ἔχοντα αὑτῶν ἄττα [53b]). And yet, one can dream of the χώρα as it was in this time; perhaps even one *must* have such a dream if anything binding is to be said of the χώρα. Indeed it will turn out that the force of the dream lies in its power to bring forth an image of the χώρα, of the χώρα as it was in the time before there were images. In the time of the dream there will be brought forth an image of the χώρα in an *autre temps* when there were not yet any images at all, or rather, as it would have been in that *autre temps*, had it been such that one could say simply that it had been, had it been such that one could then have said of it simply: it *is*.

But when it comes to the dream of the time of the χώρα, perhaps nothing can be said *simply*, perhaps nothing can *simply* be said. Derrida has, above all, called attention to the precautions that any such discourse will now have to observe, on pain of violating in its very form, in the rhetorical resources that it puts in play, the configuration determining that which, in this regard, is to be said: "Almost all the interpreters of the *Timaeus* gamble here *[misent à cet endroit]* on the resources of rhetoric without asking about them. They speak tranquilly about metaphors, images, similes. They pose no questions about this tradition of rhetoric, which places at their disposal a reserve of concepts that are very useful but that are built upon this distinction between the sensible and the intelligible, which is precisely that to which the thought of the χώρα can no longer be accommodated."[7] One will not be entitled, then, to take the resources of classical rhetoric for granted, to let discourse now on the χώρα be filled out with concepts such as that of metaphor, of simile, and of image. The same will need to be said even of concept, of the "concept" of concept, which likewise is built on the distinction between the sensible and the intelligible, the very distinction that the *Timaeus* puts into question precisely at the moment when it comes to speak of the χώρα. On the other hand, not taking any of these classical de-

7. Derrida, *Khôra*, 21.

terminations for granted does not amount simply to prohibiting them from entering a discourse now on the χώρα. But if they are to be put in play—as I have proposed putting *image* into play—their sense must in every case be determined strictly from the Platonic text itself. Even if, as in the case of *image*, this very text, the *Timaeus*, also puts this determination in question.

If in this connection one were to insist on retaining a discourse of imagination, the demands would be still more difficult. An *autre temps* in which one could not even imagine imagining: that which is in this *autre temps*—though without itself quite *being*, without quite being itself—is then in the dream to be brought forth (allowed to arrive) in the guise of an image. What must be proper to imagination (and how abysmally must it be expropriated) in order that it let arrive images of that in relation to which one cannot even imagine imagining? One suspects that this propriety would turn out to be no less strange than that alluded to in the title (and text) of a short prose piece by Beckett: "Imagination Dead Imagine."[8]

Before taking up the return to the dream as Derrida has marked it in "Tense," let me underline again the strangeness of that which—without quite being—belongs to the *autre temps*. Not that the χώρα is not also in the time after the god has fabricated both the cosmos and this time itself: yet even as it perdures in leaving its marks on the fabricated cosmos, it remains *autre*, it "*est toujours autre*." Its alterity comes to be most pointedly in question when one considers the bearing of the χώρα with respect to being. Derrida introduces such considerations explicitly in *Khôra*: "But if Timaeus names it receptacle (*dekhomenon*) or place [*lieu*] (*khôra*), these names do not designate an essence, the stable being of an *eidos*, since *khôra* is neither of the order of the *eidos* nor of the order of mimemes, of the images of the *eidos*, which come to imprint themselves on it—which thus *is not* and does not belong to the two known or recognized genera of being."[9] It should not go unnoticed that in this passage a kind of translation of the word χώρα has insinuated itself, a translation that has indeed a venerable history, going back at least to Chalcidius' Latin translation

8. Samuel Beckett, *Collected Shorter Prose 1945–1980* (London: John Calder, 1984), 145–47.

9. Derrida, *Khôra*, 28.

of the *Timaeus* in the fifth century A.D., in which χώρα is rendered as *locus*. Still, *locus* and *lieu* are translations[10] and cannot but raise interminable questions when it is a matter, as with the word χώρα (assuming it to be a word), of a word that threatens the very possibility of translation, that threatens to disrupt that detour through a common signified that has nearly always been taken to constitute translation.

Yet the focal issue in the passage—the issue I want to underline—is that of the bearing of the χώρα with respect to being. Within the discursive rhythm of the *Timaeus* the χώρα is counted—repeatedly—along with other kinds (γένη) that could be counted as kinds of being. One would say, then, of the χώρα that it is a third kind of being, counted after the first kind (intelligible) and the second kind (sensible). And yet, the designation cannot stand: for only the first kind (the intelligible εἴδη) can be called *being*, whereas the second kind is generation (γένεσις, τὸ γιγνόμενον), and the third kind is the *in which* (τὸ ἐν ᾧ) or the receptacle (ὑποδοχή) of all generation. If the second kind can be said to have some slight share in being, so that a sensible thing can be called *a being*, there would seem to be little or no possibility of extending such a name to the third kind. It is neither being nor a being, neither an intelligible being nor a sensible being; as Derrida says, it "does not belong to the two known or recognized genera of being." If it is a being in any sense whatsoever, then it would have to be so in a sense of being beyond being, in a sense of being in excess of being. Even if, short of venturing to think such excess, one were to say that it is nothing, an immediate qualification, a kind of retraction, would be required, as in a recent text where Derrida writes: "Khôra is nothing (nothing of being or of present), but not the Nothing that, in Dasein's anxiety, would open again to the question of being."[11] From being it is even more remote,

10. In a more recent text Derrida seems to insist even on this translation, though surrounding it with precautions and exclusions that serve to ward off many of the ghosts that otherwise would haunt it so incessantly as to make the word χώρα, as it operates in the *Timaeus*, virtually unreadable in a word such as *lieu*. Still: "Khôra . . . would be, at least according to the interpretation that I have ventured of it, the name of place [*le nom de lieu*], *a* name of place . . ." ("Foi et savoir: Les deux sources de la 'religion' aux limites de la simple raison," in *La Religion* [Séminaire de Capri sous la direction de Jacques Derrida et Gianni Vattimo] [Paris: Éditions du Seuil, 1996], 31).

11. Ibid.

more alien, than every nothing that still, however obliquely, opens onto being. The χώρα remains other, *elle est toujours autre*.

In "Tense" Derrida recalls the phrase with which being in excess of being is most forcefully expressed in the Platonic text, a phrase that has been taken up and made to play an important role by Heidegger and Levinas, the phrase that Plato reserves for what (in the interest of economy) can be translated as *the good*: the phrase is ἐπέκεινα τῆς οὐσίας, *beyond being*. Recalling this phrase, Derrida asks about its pertinence as regards the χώρα, that is, whether the phrase is suitable for saying the relevant excess. He asks, in particular, why it happens that Plato does not use the phrase in this way: "And yet why does not Plato say that χώρα is ἐπέκεινα τῆς οὐσίας? Why is that so difficult to say and to think?"[12] Elsewhere, even more forcefully, no longer in the form of a question, he writes: "Khộra . . . does not even announce itself as 'beyond being' ['*au-delà de l'être*']."[13]

It is as if there were a double excess, or rather, not *a* double but two excesses, two ways of being beyond being, two ways that would be themselves unrelated, uncrossed, without even a moment of coincidence sufficient to allow the phrase ἐπέκεινα τῆς οὐσίας to be extended from one to the other. In posing the question of this double excess in which each would also seem absolutely to exceed the other, Derrida has opened an immense domain of questions; and they are questions of the utmost pertinence for the effort today to think the limit of metaphysics, to think being at the limit of metaphysics.

In this regard I will restrict myself to a single point, to a mere indication of one point—among many, no doubt—from which one might develop certain of the questions belonging to this domain opened up by Derrida's texts on the *Timaeus*. But even before marking that point, let me call attention to the passage in Book 6 of the *Republic* in which Socrates speaks of the good in its peculiar excess. It is a matter of declaring, first of all, that the to-be and being (τὸ εἶναι τε καὶ τὴν οὐσίαν) belong to things on account of the good; and then that "the good is not being but is still beyond being [ἐπέκεινα τῆς οὐσίας], exceeding it [ὑπερέχοντος] in dignity and power" (*Rep.* 509b). One presumes that the power (δύναμις) of the good by which

12. Derrida, "Tense," 73.

13. Derrida, "Foi et savoir," 31.

it exceeds being lies in its being empowered to bestow being upon whatever is, to bring being to belong to things. But its excess is not only one of power but also of dignity. Without venturing to suppose what might constitute the dignity of the good in this ontological connection, what dignity could conceivably signify here, let me merely note that πρεσβεία, which one readily translates as *dignity*, also means *age* or *seniority*. The verb πρεσβεύω can mean, among other things: to take the place of others by right of seniority, to rule over others by virtue of being the oldest. The good is older than being, and it rules over all beings by first bestowing upon them their being. The good is anterior to being and beings; it belongs to a time before being and beings, an *autre temps*.

In any case one should not overlook the very remarkable response that Glaucon offers to Socrates' declaration about the excessiveness of the good: "And Glaucon, quite ridiculously, said, 'Apollo, what a demonic excess'" (*Rep*. 509c).

What, then, about the relation—or even nonrelation—between the excess of the good and that of the χώρα? As Derrida notes, Plato's text makes no direct reference to such a relation; or, more precisely, it never extends to the χώρα the designation ἐπέκεινα τῆς οὐσίας. And yet, there is a point—and this is the one I want to mark—where the good and the χώρα are brought into a very remarkable proximity. This point comes in the passage at the beginning of Book 7 of the *Republic* where Socrates speaks of "our nature in its education and lack of education" by asking Glaucon to imagine an underground cavelike dwelling and its inhabitants who, though initially bound, come to be released and to ascend into the openness and the light above. Toward the end of the passage, Socrates speaks of what sounds like a culmination of the ascent: from looking at reflections of things in water, the liberated prisoner could come to look at things themselves and then could turn his gaze upward so as to behold things in the heaven and the heaven itself, more easily at night, looking at the light of the stars and the moon. Socrates concludes: "Then finally I suppose he would be able to look upon the sun—not its appearances [its phantoms—φαντάσματα] in water or in some other base [ἕδρα], but the sun itself by itself in its own χώρα—and behold how it is" (*Rep*. 516b).

In the commentary that Socrates conjoins to the entire passage, he correlates the various sites and stages with those already delimited in Book 6 with respect to the affections in the soul and the corresponding levels of disclosure of beings.[14] On the basis of this correlation, together with the earlier parallel by which the sun is said to be "an offspring the good begot in proportion [ἀνάλογον] with itself" (*Rep.* 508b–c), one can carry over what is said of the sun into something to be said of the good. Here it is not a matter of drawing uncritically on the traditional rhetorical concept of metaphor but of recognizing that this is one of those points in the Platonic texts—perhaps even the single most decisive one—where the very sense of metaphor comes to be established, where the very domains are first conjoined between which metaphors will, from that point on, transport sense into sense: "as the good is in the intelligible region [ἐν τῷ νοητῷ τόπῳ] with respect to intelligence [νοῦς] and what is intellected, so the sun is in the visible region with respect to sight and what is seen" (*Rep.* 508c).

What, then, of the χώρα and of the proximity of its excess to that of the good? The connection is clear enough in the case of the good's offspring. In this case the proximity is linked to the propriety of the sun: it is precisely when one no longer sees its phantoms, precisely when one looks at it itself by itself (αὐτὸν καθ' αὑτόν), when one sees the sun proper—it is precisely then that one sees it in its χώρα. Thus, to see it in its χώρα is not at all to see it in relation to something else rather than as itself and by itself; on the contrary, seeing it as itself by itself *is* precisely seeing it in its χώρα. Only in its χώρα does the sun come to be beheld properly, as itself and by itself.

Especially in those passages where attention turns to the apparent culmination of the ascent, Socrates almost invariably inserts disclaimers, reservations, references to opinion and to how things seem, all of which serve to divert or defer the movement he is describing or feigning to describe.[15] For example, in the midst of describing the ascent to the intelligible region, he abruptly inserts the following remarks before then going on to speak of the good: "A god doubtless knows if it chances to be true. At all events this is how the appearance appears to me" (*Rep.* 517b). But even apart from such strategies,

14. I have discussed these passages of the *Republic* in detail in *Being and Logos*, 401–43.

15. See my discussion in *Delimitations*, chapter 1.

questions cannot but accumulate around what Socrates says of the sun in its χώρα. Not the least among them is the question of blindness: for one could look upon the sun itself by itself, beholding it in its χώρα, only at the risk of blindness. In another celebrated passage Socrates cites this risk as precisely what provoked his turn from things to λόγοι, his δεύτερος πλοῦς (*Phaedo* 99d–e). Does the χώρα also pose such a risk, at least in its proximity to the sun proper? Is there, then, provocation to turn from vision to λόγος? Furthermore, what about the metaphorical move, the translating of the vision of the sun over into the intellection or hyper-intellection of the good? What happens to the χώρα in this translation? Can the χώρα be carried over from the sensible to the intelligible, even though, as the *Timaeus* demonstrates, it is neither sensible nor intelligible? Can there be, then, a metaphorizing of the χώρα? If not, then how is one to read the passage on the χώρα of the sun, that is, how is one to read it within the metaphorics explicitly established in this very context? How—through what kind of translation—is the χώρα of the sun to be carried over into the χώρα of the good? Is there a χώρα of the good? And is the good to be looked upon itself by itself precisely when it is beheld in its χώρα? What is required in order to behold the good in its χώρα? How is the χώρα itself—if there be a χώρα *itself*—to be beheld?

How is the χώρα to be apprehended? How is it to be perceived, assuming that some sense of perception is pertinent to its apprehension?

In a dream. The χώρα is to be apprehended in a dream.

Or as in a dream. This precisely is what Derrida says, what he ascribes to Plato, though one will want to add that what is said in this regard comes in the voice of Timaeus.

In a dream. Or as in a dream. What is the difference marked by the *as*? Does it express only some vague similarity between the state of dreaming and that in which one would apprehend the χώρα? Or is the dream integral to such apprehension so that the *as* would mark only a certain distancing, a hermeneutic interval? Derrida observes, in any case, that this apprehension, linked somehow to a dream, is thereby exposed to two contrary effects: it "could just as well deprive it of lucidity as confer upon it a power of divination."[16]

16. Derrida, *Khôra*, 17.

Here it must suffice merely to indicate these two contrary moments.

The reference to the dream comes in a passage at the center of the *Timaeus*, the passage in which this third kind finally comes to be called χώρα. This passage (*Tim.* 52a–d) I call the *chorology*. Timaeus tells exactly how the χώρα is to be apprehended: it is "to be apprehended, with nonsensation [μετ' ἀναισθησίας], by a sort of bastard reckoning [λογισμῷ τινὶ νόθῳ]" (*Tim.* 52b). Thus, it is not to be apprehended by perception, if the sense of perception is determined by the traditional connection to αἴσθησις, that is, if it is taken as sense-perception. Yet this does not entail that the apprehension of the χώρα is a matter of intellectual or noetic vision (νόησις). On the contrary, just as the introduction of the χώρα puts in question the very opposition between αισθητόν and νοητόν, so likewise its apprehension is not such as can be confined to this opposition and its field.

It is just at the point where the apprehension is called bastard reckoning, something "hardly trustworthy," that Timaeus refers to the dream of the χώρα: "And looking toward which we dream [of it] and affirm that it is necessary that all that is be somewhere in some place [τόπος] and occupy [but also, putting the double sense of κατέχον in play: hold back from, be withheld from] some χώρα; and that that which is neither on earth nor anywhere in the heavens is nothing" (*Tim.* 52b).

In the dream the χώρα is pictured as the place in which all that is must be. In the oneiric vision the χώρα—or rather, its dream-image—hovers before us as a place so all-encompassing that whatever is set apart from it can only be nothing. But what is there in a dream? Socrates tells Glaucon what there is in a dream, tells him through a series of questions posed in a passage in Book 5 of the *Republic*: "Is the man who holds that there are beautiful things but does not hold that there is beauty itself and who, if someone leads him to the knowledge of it, is not able to follow—is he, in your opinion, living in a dream or is he awake? Consider it. Does dreaming, whether one is asleep or awake, not consist in believing a likeness of something to be not a likeness but rather the thing itself to which it is like?" (*Rep.* 476c). Glaucon agrees that such a man is dreaming, and Socrates then goes on to contrast the dreamer with a man who believes that there is a beautiful itself and who is able to distinguish between it and its images, the many beautiful things. Glaucon agrees that the latter man is quite awake. Formalizing, one could say: to dream is to be aware only of images, without recognizing the images *as* images, hence without distinguishing them from their original. To dream is to be completely caught up with images, to be oblivious to those things of which they are images.

What, then, about the dream of the χώρα? What are the images in which we remain caught up? What are the distinctions to which we are blind?

In the dream, deprived by it of lucidity, we "affirm that it is necessary that all that is be somewhere in some place [τόπος] and occupy some χώρα." The word τόπος can of course be translated as *place*; one might presume even that it was partly because of this very passage that χώρα too came to be translated as *locus* (Chalcidius) and then as *place* (Thomas Taylor). But in texts prior to the Aristotelian determination of τόπος it is more appropriate to render τόπος as something like *region*. Even Aristotle, though fixing a precise sense, still uses the word in this sense, dividing the entire universe into three τόποι.[17] What is operative in such division is the intrinsic connection made in Greek thought between specific regions and what, from Aristotle on (though not yet in Plato), are called the elements; the upper region is that of fire and aether, the lower that of earth. In fact, just after the chorology there is a passage that makes this connection explicit: "The greater part of each kind keeps apart in a region [τόπος] of its own because of the movement of the recipient" (57c). Thus, in failing to make the distinction between χώρα and τόπος, conflating them by mere coordination, as in the passage, one fails to distinguish between the χώρα and its appearance as, for instance, a fiery region.[18] In the dream one simply pictures the χώρα as a kind of region of regions in which all things would have their place. Hence, one conflates the χώρα and τόπος; one fails to distinguish between the χώρα and its appearance, even though this appearing is not a matter of casting an image. For in the *autre temps* of the χώρα there are no images, only traces of fire, air, water, and earth.

17. Aristotle, *Progression of Animals* 706b.

18. Just before the chorology Timaeus speaks of the peculiar appearing of the χώρα: "That part of it that is made fiery appears as fire" (*Tim.* 51b). Immediately following the chorology there is another, similar reference to such appearing (see *Tim.* 52d–e). My text "Of the Χώρα" is largely oriented to the question of this appearing. See also my discussion in *Chorology*, 109.

In the dream there is also an equally decisive conflation of the intelligible and the sensible, even though in the *autre temps* of the χώρα the sensible has still to become itself, that is, still consists only of fugitive traces. The dream vision is of a region in which all that is would be placed, whereas one who awakens from the dream will—as Timaeus goes on to say—recognize that the intelligible εἴδη are set apart, that they do not pass anywhere else into another. To awaken from the dream would be, then, to come to distinguish the three kinds conflated in the oneiric vision, to come to count them off in their distinctness, reenacting the opening words of the dialogue: *one, two, three.*

But in the dream something is received, as if conferred by some power of divination. Even though in the dream one fails to distinguish between the three kinds, still something is *disclosed* in the dream, namely, that of which one dreams, the χώρα. Furthermore, awakening from the dream, one can then draw those proper distinctions that were lacking in the oneiric vision: Timaeus demonstrates this in deed by going on to say the truth that one would say upon awakening, telling how it is that by virtue of the χώρα images, sensible things, first come to be[19]—to the extent that it can be told and to the extent that they come *to be* (rather than being nothing at all). Thus, he tells how the χώρα is the site where a new time begins, a time other than the *autre temps* of the χώρα. But he can tell of this time of images only by telling—if more distinctly—about the dream-image of that *autre temps* when there were yet no images but only the fugitive traces of things not yet themselves.

Much later in the dialogue Timaeus speaks of the liver. What he says makes it clear that the liver is a kind of reproduction of the χώρα within the human body. Timaeus says that it is made smooth and bright so that "the power of thoughts that proceed from intellect [νοῦς] move in the liver as in a mirror that receives impressions and provides visible images" (*Tim.* 71b). It is then around the liver that a part of the soul "in the night passes its time sensibly, being occupied in its slumbers with divination [μαντεία], since it does not partake of λόγος or φρόνησις" (*Tim.* 71d). Thus, there is in the lower parts of soul and body an organ of divination, a gift that the god gave to man's foolishness. One undergoes divination only when one's intellect is

19. See my discussion in "Of the Χώρα," 7–9. Also *Chorology*, 122–24.

fettered in sleep or distraught by disease or by divine inspiration (διά τινα ἐνθουσιασμόν). But, says Timaeus, "it belongs to a man when in his right senses [ἔμφρονος] to recollect and ponder the things spoken in dream or waking vision by the divining and inspired nature" (*Tim.* 71e).

Awakening to the light of day, Timaeus will thus have interpreted the dream, pondering it while still no doubt finding himself carried away by it, dreaming it again but now in daytime.

It is as if night, *l'autre nuit*, Hades itself, were to be drawn up into the light of day. One could not hope to do so except by also leaving it in the depth, keeping one's back to it, as Orpheus could hope to lead Eurydice out of Hades only by not looking back at her. Yet we know that Orpheus did not submit to this necessity: the moment he stepped out into daylight, he turned his gaze back upon her only to see her, because of his excessive act, slipping back into the darkness. This is, in the words of Blanchot, "an infinitely problematical movement, which the day condemns as unjustifiable madness"[20]—the madness of the day.

Can it be otherwise with a daydream? With a daydream of the χώρα?

---

20. Blanchot, *L'Espace littéraire*, 229. See also *La folie du jour* (Fata morgana, 1973) and Derrida's related text "La loi du genre," in *Parages* (Paris: Galilée, 1986), 249–87.

CHAPTER 4

PLATONISM AT THE LIMIT OF METAPHYSICS

THE LAST DISCUSSION I HAD with Reiner Schürmann concerned Platonism. The discussion was occasioned by a lecture[1] at the New School for Social Research in which I undertook to show how certain Platonic texts inscribe a kind of limit that would be precisely a limit of kinds, hence of the metaphysics of selfsame kinds that one otherwise takes these texts simply to have founded. The operation of such a limit has the effect of exposing Platonic thought to a primal contamination, opening it to an unassimilable alterity at the very moment when, founding what will be called metaphysics, it would declare the hegemony of the same, of what is one and the same. Such alterity is thought in the *Timaeus* as what is called the third kind, though it would be, of necessity, a kind of kind beyond kinds: Timaeus' name for it is χώρα.

In the lecture my specific concern was to mark the operation of such a limit in the Platonic discourse woven around ποίησις, especially in discourses such as that of the *Republic* in which the consti-

1. "The Politics of the Χώρα" was presented at the Hannah Arendt Memorial Symposium on Political Philosophy organized by Reiner Schürmann at the New School for Social Research in March 1991. The text of this lecture was first published in *Ancients and Moderns*, ed. Reginald Lilly (Bloomington: Indiana University Press, 1996). An expanded version of this lecture appears above as chapter 2.

tution of the πόλις is, at least at a certain level, essentially determined by reference to ποίησις, the πόλις thus being constituted, in the first instance, as a mere community of artisans. The discussion centered on the foreign, on whether a πόλις thus constituted could enter into relation to the foreign πόλις or whether, on the contrary, the alterity of the foreign would render any such relation itself foreign to such a πόλις. The discussion thus touched not only on our long-shared interest in Platonism and its relation to the limit of metaphysics but also on certain decisive questions raised in and by Hannah Arendt's critique of Western political thought as essentially utopian.

For the force of Reiner Schürmann's questions and the intensity of his response, no expression of gratitude can suffice—not even the attempt to continue the discussion by turning now, as one must, to what he wrote about Platonism. Even if one would forgo simply reinvoking the privilege of living speech over what remains in writing, one will not easily forget how Reiner Schürmann's rare voice could sweep across a text, whether his own or another's, clearing a space in which its silence might resound, as a thunderstorm can sweep away the mist and haze, leaving the air so brilliantly clear that the contours of all things radiate with rare intensity.

His was indeed a singular voice: when he spoke, it was as if his voice were cast into a desert and as if, listening from any spot on this lonely—if densely inhabited—expanse, from any point in this space of utter solitude, one received the whole voice and yet not the whole. This scene of pure singularity comes from Plotinus.[2] In his text it is the scene of the transcendence of the one, which in its utter singularity—a singularity that Reiner Schürmann never ceases to underline—exceeds immeasurably what Plotinus calls νοῦς; since νοῦς (let us say, cautiously, *intellect*) marks the limit of being, this transcendence is such as to render the one "beyond being," in the phrase that Plotinus takes over from the *Republic* and reinscribes throughout the *Enneads*. This reinscription and indeed the depiction of the scene of transcendence that I have just reinscribed indicate to what extent the Plotinian discourse on singularity is haunted by spacings; these still preliminary indications will make it less surprising that at a decisive

2. *Enneads* III.8.9. Subsequent references to this work will be given in the text as *Enn.*

point this discourse will be developed as a discourse on spacing, on the spacing of the utterly singular, the spacing of the one.

As to spacing as such—note that I do not say the *concept* of spacing, nor could I beyond a point continue to compensate by adding the *as such*—let me stress its anteriority, which mitigates somewhat the foreignness that it would otherwise have to Plotinian thought: what is called spacing is constituted prior to the distinction between sensible and intelligible and thus refers indifferently both to the configuration of things in space and to the differentiating relations between intelligibles. Moreover, spacing is not simply reducible to the concept of difference, if for no other reason than that it is meant to invoke what comes into play in the Timaean discourse that I have already mentioned, the discourse on the χώρα. I shall have to indicate precisely the sense of this invocation by locating a point in Plotinus' discourse on the transcendence of the one where it becomes necessary to bring into play something like the Platonic chorology.

But, first of all, it is a matter of another spacing, of bringing it to bear on an identity proposed by Heidegger, of setting apart the terms of the proposed identity, of opening between them a space of reservation, the space of a certain reserve. Heidegger proposes the identity in the formula: "Metaphysics is Platonism."[3] The prospect of spacing this identity is posed as soon as one simply reverses it and puts the reverse in question. Can it be said equally that Platonism is metaphysics? Is Platonism simply metaphysics? Is Platonism the instance of metaphysics that founds and determines all subsequent metaphysics as such? Is it a kind of original metaphysics, the original kind of metaphysics, the original that founds and determines all kinds of metaphysics? Is this why metaphysics is Platonism? Because Platonism is its origin, an ἀρχή from which it never essentially departs?

Or is there in this origin a reserve, something held back from the metaphysics that it founds and determines, something withheld from all subsequent thought precisely to the degree that such thought remains metaphysical? Would such a reserve not twist against the very metaphysics that the Platonic original would found and determine? Would it not effect a certain transgression of the limit of metaphysics at the very origin of metaphysics? Would it not produce, in Heidegger's

3. Heidegger, *Zur Sache des Denkens*, 63.

phrase, an overcoming of metaphysics at the very inception of metaphysics, at the very moment of inception? And could such a reserve not recur and produce the same effect in the thought of one who powerfully reinscribes the original metaphysics?

In the thought of Plotinus such transgressive reserve has its locus in henology, in the discourse on the one. It is just such reserve that Reiner Schürmann undertakes to retrieve in his paper "Neoplatonic Henology as an Overcoming of Metaphysics," published in 1983.[4] In this paper he draws a contrast between a prospective reading of the texts belonging to the Neoplatonic tradition and their retrospective reading. The first, more traditional type of reading is attentive to intrinsic development and continuity, while the other type returns to that tradition across a "fusion of horizons," revealing its breaks or ruptures. In a prospective reading of the Neoplatonic texts, henology appears as negative theology: the discourse would be determined by an identification of the one as the supreme being, as a being "*inconceivably* actual, spiritual, changeless, powerful, causative, eternal" (*NH*, 30). Because the one, as supreme being, would transcend our limited concepts, discourse on the one could mark this transcendence only by negation of these limited concepts. In his later work Schürmann introduces the term *maximization* to designate what is operative in the construal of henology as negative theology: the one is taken as that being in which are maximized all the positive attributes conceivable to us as such but inconceivable in their maximization.

On the other hand, a retrospective reading such as Schürmann wants to pursue insists that the one is not a being, not even a supreme being whose attributes might escape the grasp of the limited human intellect, indeed not even a supreme being whose very being would be beyond being as conceived by the human intellect. Whatever is a being—even if in a sense inconceivable to us—must, as Schürmann puts it, "rank, for that very reason, *after* some more radical condition" (*NH*, 31). Schürmann cites a later Neoplatonist, the so-called "Anonymous of Turino," who says even that the one "is itself the 'to be' [τὸ εἶναι]" (*NH*, 31). On this basis Schürmann proposes, then, a correlation with the grammatical form of the participle, which participates

4. "Neoplatonic Henology as an Overcoming of Metaphysics," *Research in Phenomenology* 13 (1983), 25–41. Subsequent references are given in the text as *NH*.

in both the verb and the noun: the radical condition, the one, would correspond to the verbal function, while what comes after it—for example, the intellect—would correspond to the nominal function. Thus, *being* would be unlimited in its range of application, but only on the condition that its application to the one be restricted to the verbal form; otherwise it will simply have to be said, as Plotinus himself does throughout the *Enneads*, that the one is beyond being, that the first being is the intellect, that, in Schürmann's phrase, the radical condition preceding that first being is not-being.

The correlation in terms of grammatical form prepares the way for a more philosophically decisive correlation. Schürmann proposes a correlation that borders on interpretive identification, namely, with the Heideggerian ontological difference. The difference between the one and what comes after it, the henological difference, as Schürmann later calls it, is construed as the difference between *das Sein* and *das Seiende*. In this connection one begins to realize that in spacing the Heideggerian identity, in loosening and complicating the bond between Platonism and metaphysics, it is never, for Schürmann, a matter of diminishing the force of Heidegger's thought. Not only does Heidegger's thought first make possible something like Schürmann's retrospective reading, opening the very dimension of such a reading, freeing the space of its questions; but it also provides the resources to which Schürmann repeatedly turns in his efforts to think the transgressive reserve in Plotinian thought in a way that avoids reinscribing it in metaphysics in and through the very movement of delimiting it. Thus he undertakes to think the Plotinian one verbally, as unification, though without any substantial agent whose act such unification would be. The Plotinian one would be, says Schürmann, "the factor of coordination in all things," "their entrance into an order of interconnectedness"; it would be "the very movement . . . of coming-to-presence in all that there is" (*NH*, 33). Schürmann poses the word with which Heidegger, in his distinctive way, would think beyond being, the untranslatable *Ereignis*. And yet, however much Plotinus may be regarded as having already thought in the direction that *Ereignis* would name, Schürmann stops short of identifying the Plotinian one with what Heidegger, using the word as a *singulare tantum*,[5] calls *Ereignis*.

5. Heidegger, *Identität und Differenz* (Pfullingen: Günther Neske, 1957), 29.

Hence, while continuing to insist that Plotinus' henology has "effectively overcome metaphysics," Schürmann adds the cautionary qualification: "if only by the slightest edge" (*NH*, 35). Indeed, he is explicit about the nonidentification: "I am not claiming that the medieval henologists understood being, in the verbal sense, the way Heidegger understands *Ereignis*. Their lack of a sense for history should suffice to prevent anyone from such syncretism" (*NH*, 33).

But what, then, is he claiming, granted that such syncretism is to be avoided? He continues: "I am suggesting, however, that the medieval henologists were the ones who most clearly, in the Western tradition, thought of the difference between being as a process and being as substance" (*NH*, 33f.). Yet, one cannot but wonder how much weight can be borne by such an opposition, that between process and substance. One cannot but wonder what would be required in order to prevent this opposition from reverting almost immediately to the guise in which it has run its course *within* metaphysics, at least from Hegel through Whitehead. And one cannot but wonder how much can be accomplished by going on to explicate this opposition by alignment with the Heideggerian differentiation between *Anwesen* and *Anwesenheit*. Would not such an interpretive alignment, in order to give transgressive force to the otherwise metaphysical opposition between process and substance, have to draw the interpretation so thoroughly into the orbit of Heidegger's thought that again, if referred back to Plotinus, it could not but appear syncretic?

In view of this hermeneutical aporia, it is hardly surprising that toward the end of his paper Schürmann's reinscriptions of Plotinian henology become largely negative, that is, focused on differentiating the one from, as he says, any "ultimate ground for anchoring all our endeavors, whether theoretical or practical" (*NH*, 34). What can be learned from Neoplatonic henology is, then, the renunciation of the search for some ultimate authority, for a final, measure-giving ground. Whatever is a being, however ultimate, however supreme, however measure-giving, ranks for that very reason after another that is not a being, after the one; and however final such a being may be taken to be, it has finally to be renounced in order that contemplation (θεωρία) be drawn to what is absolutely first. The question is whether such renunciation is a renunciation *of ground*. For how otherwise is ground to be understood than as ἀρχή? How otherwise than by way of the translation that Heidegger himself proposes, the translation of *Grund* as ἀρχή?[6] But in this case the dissociation of the one from ground will be inhibited, perhaps even, finally, impossible. For in Plotinus' text there is hardly anything more consistently said of the one than that it is the ἀρχή, the ground or origin of all things, of everything that can be called a being.

In his massive final work, *Broken Hegemonies*, Schürmann takes up again the reading of the Plotinian texts developed in the earlier paper. The earlier perspective is still quite recognizable: it is still a matter of the henological overcoming of metaphysics or, as he now formulates it, a matter of dismounting or unframing (*désencadre*) Plotinian henology from metaphysics. But now, in *Broken Hegemonies*, the reading of Plotinus is set within a context that is both systematically articulated and extended across the entire history of metaphysics, stretching from Parmenides to Heidegger by way of Augustine, Eckhart, Luther, and Kant. Plato, too, belongs now to the context, even if less systematically than the other figures just mentioned. Indeed, it is by marking what seems to be an advance beyond Plato that Schürmann introduces Plotinus' exorbitant henology: "By thus upholding the incognizability and the non-being of the One, henology turns Plato against himself. With Plato, Plotinus holds that to be is to be intelligible. But against Plato, he discovers that when we speak of things intelligible we always speak of multiple things, be it only of the duality of knowing and known. Now, nothing which implies otherness—or, even more so, multiplicity—can be First. Intelligence and being will be derivatives because they are intrinsically multiple. This is why, in the Plotinian universe, no being can claim ultimacy. Thus, if it is due to the One that all beings are beings, the One is not itself to be found among them."[7] Here, as in the earlier paper, Schürmann underlines the detachment of the one from being and from intelligibility, hence also from the intellect, which comes to know the intelligible. Because it tolerates neither multiplicity nor otherness of any kind, the one is set completely outside the orbit of that which is. Being exorbitant, it is apart from all beings, utterly alone, solitary.

---

6. Heidegger, *Die Metaphysik des deutschen Idealismus (Schelling)*, vol. 49 of *Gesamtausgabe* (Frankfurt a.M.: Vittorio Klostermann, 1991), 77.

7. Reiner Schürmann, *Des Hégémonies Brisées* (Mauvezin: Trans-Europ-Repress, 1996), 186–87. Subsequent references are given in the text as *HB*.

But now, in *Broken Hegemonies*, Schürmann deploys a richer discourse in his effort to reinscribe Plotinian henology in its exorbitance. Not only can the one be said to owe nothing to the maximizing mechanics operative in negative theology; it can also be declared void of all content to which such mechanics could be applied. In Schürmann's unqualified words: the One is "without content" (*HB*, 187). It is, he says, not a thesis, but a centering (*centrage*), one which centers all things. One will still want to ask what it means to be a centering—even while recognizing the daunting instability of such a question about the meaning of the being of something that is utterly outside meaning, i.e., intelligibility, and being. To say nothing of the aporetic figure of an exorbitant centering, of a centering from beyond the periphery.

The discourse already deployed in the earlier paper continues to be developed in *Broken Hegemonies*. Schürmann refers to the henological difference and to the necessity of differentiating it from the metaphysical difference between οὐσία and ὄν, or, in Heidegger's idiom, between *die Seiendheit* and *das Seiende*. Distinguishing the one from a "supreme ground" that would be "a plenary real," he calls it now, in one passage at least, "the transcendental condition of appearing" (*HB*, 190). One would have to insist that such a conception be made to pass quite outside the familiar orbit in which it was established by Kant, that it no longer be thought as an interior transcendental ground by which the subject would ground all appearing. Rather, it must be a transcendental ground utterly recast in the guise, as Schürmann says, of "a singular event of union" in which beings "enter into a constellation" and thus first become the beings they are (*HB*, 191). He calls it also "the self-configuring by virtue of which . . . there are figures." Or again: "the pure entrance of things into constellation" (*HB*, 193). In perhaps the most compact formulation: "The One is manifestation" (*HB*, 204).

The most radical move ventured in Schürmann's reading of Plotinus in *Broken Hegemonies* has to do with time, with raising, as he says, "the most arduous question—heretical within the Neoplatonic tradition—of the temporality of the One" (*HB*, 196). What he takes to be most radical in Plotinus' thinking of time are not, as often supposed, those elements by which Plotinus anticipates Augustine's discourse in Book 11 of the *Confessions*, namely, the *distentio* into past, present, and future, which Plotinus calls διάστασις, and the assimilation of time to the soul, its interiorization (see *Enn.* III.7.11). Schürmann is explicit: "Interiority cannot be Plotinus' last word about time" (*HB*, 200). His last word has rather to do with originary time, with the time of the origin. But the origin is just the one, Schürmann now bringing into play the discourse, held back heretofore, on the one as ἀρχή. Since the time, as it were, of the intelligible and the intellect is eternity, Plotinus' last word about time would be a discourse on that time of which eternity would be an image, thus inverting the well-known formula from the *Timaeus*. Yet, the time of the one cannot be anything other than the one, nor either of these anything other than the origin. Thus, following much the same path that Heidegger set out upon when, at the outset of *Being and Time*, he proposed to thematize the temporality of Being (*Temporalität des Seins*), Schürmann's passage through the question of the temporality of the one comes around, in the end, to the unification, the movement of coming-to-presence, by which the one has been characterized all along. But now, this movement is taken as originary time itself: "the very matter, *die Sache selbst*, of henology is the entering of a multitude of factors into a constellation, the 'coming-to-be' of such a constellation: in other words, originary time" (*HB*, 205).

One cannot but have some reservations about bringing into play such Heideggerian resources in order to think the transgressive reserve of Plotinian henology. No doubt, by proceeding from what Heidegger's thought has opened up, carrying out what Schürmann calls a retrospective reading, one can gain an otherwise unlikely access to Plotinus' texts, especially with regard to the dimension in which they exceed metaphysics by posing the discourse on the one outside the metaphysical discourse circulating between intelligible and sensible. And yet, gaining such access, one could rigorously reinscribe the Plotinian discourse touching on this dimension only by forgoing the syncretism that would massively import Heideggerian resources into the reinscription. At the very least—and Schürmann acknowledged this with complete candor—the proximity of the Heideggerian resources must be rigorously limited and those resources made to bear on Plotinus' text only from a certain distance, operating across that distance only by action of an affinity irreducible to an interpretive identity.

There is also another possibility, a kind of reading that might come to augment or at least to supplement the necessarily limited capacity of a retrospective reading. This other reading would be neither retrospective nor prospective but in a sense both at the same time, returning to Plotinus' text in the manner of a retrospective reading and yet bringing to bear on the reinscription of that text, not resources belonging to the thought of our time, but resources belonging to Platonism from its inception. Yet at the moment of reinscription this other reading would not simply become prospective; rather it would be a matter of activating in the reinscription something that, at best, was only concealedly in play in Platonism, something broached in Plato's texts that was, for the most part, held back from Platonism, a reserve of another kind.

Here only a few indications can be given regarding one such other reading. In this case the reading will be oriented to spacing, this orientation expressing already the double-directedness of such a reading, granted what was said about spacing at the outset, especially about the Platonic context that it is meant to invoke.

Still, one will say that if it is heretical within Neoplatonism to raise the question of the temporality of the one, it is even more heretical to raise the question of the spacing of the one. Indeed it would be not only heretical but downright nonsensical, *if* spacing were to designate only the spatial configuring of things in space, for then spacing would be confined to the merely sensible domain; it could have no bearing on the soul or the intellect, much less on the one. Yet, in Schürmann's reading there is already a discourse on a configuring, a coming into constellation, that is not at all reducible to the mere establishing of spatial relations between sensible things. On the contrary, such configuring is not only linked to the one but is virtually identified as the one. Clearly, then, since the one is the ἀρχή of *all* things, its configuring would have to extend across the intelligible as well as the sensible. This convergence of the two discourses—on spacing and on configuring, respectively—suggests that spacing is not to be simply opposed to time or temporalization and that, correspondingly, the relation between the two readings is more intimate and complex than one might have supposed.

Indeed Plotinus himself authorizes a certain spatially-determined discourse, extending it explicitly beyond the sensible. Thus, one is to say that soul and intellect are *outside* the whole cosmos (τοῦ παντὸς οὐρανοῦ ἔξω); one can say too that soul and intellect are in ourselves, but they belong to us not insofar as we are beings of the sensible order but insofar as we are *outside* the sensible, just as soul and intellect as such are outside the sensible. According a certain legitimation to a discourse of inside and outside, even when the discourse concerns what is not at all sensible, Plotinus also indicates that such discourse requires a certain semantic modification—one could be tempted to call it a metaphorizing—when it is extended beyond the sensible. Thus, referring to the reasoning part of the soul, he says: "For we should not look for a place [τόπος] in which to put it, but make it exist outside all place [ἔξω τόπου παντός]" (*Enn.* V.1.10). Most remarkably, his very insistence on modifying the spatially-determined discourse when it is extended beyond the sensible is itself an instance of spatially-determined discourse: what does not have a place in the sensible domain is said to be *outside* all place.

Yet, for a reading set on exposing and reinscribing the henological excess, the primary concern is not with the spacing of beings, not even of the highest beings, but with the spacing of the one, with the spacing by which the one is—as Plotinus says again and again—alone, solitary, separate, set apart, turned always to itself. Plotinus never ceases to remark on the difficulty of discoursing on the solitary one—for instance: "No wonder it is not easy to say, when it is not even easy to say being and form." As one approaches the one, he explains, one goes toward the formless (ἀνείδεον), which, because it is not delimited, resists comprehension, letting one slide past as if it were nothing at all. Even to say: *That one is in itself*—even here it is necessary to take back something of what is said, both the "that" and the "is." Rather than snaring it in the discourse, one only runs round it outside (ἔξωθεν) (*Enn.* VI.9.3). Its spacing is such as to make the discourse on it recoil and circulate at a certain aporetic distance.

Yet the spacing of the one is not only a matter of its separation, however unmodified, unqualified, that separation may remain. For the one is the ἀρχή of all things: "It is by the one that all beings are beings" (*Enn.* VI.9.1). The resultant complexity of its spacing is expressed when Plotinus says that it is everywhere and nowhere., It is everywhere, there is nowhere where it is not, it fills all things, for it is that by which all beings are beings. But if it were only everywhere, it would also *be* all things—that is, if it were not also withdrawn, lonely and apart, before all things, nowhere (*Enn.* III.9.4).

When Plotinus' text turns to the one, it tends, then, to stress the more aporetic separation and lays out repeatedly a series of differentiations pertinent to the apartness of the one. First and most globally, the one is differentiated from all things. It is before all things (πρὸ τῶν πάντων), before them as the ἀρχή from which they come; hence, it is not all nor any one of them (*Enn.* III.8.9). For if it were all things—or even, one might add, any one of them in addition to being the ἀρχή—then it would no longer be one but many—at least two. On the other hand, the others—that is, all things—are established by it, or, as one could also translate ἵδρυται, situated, placed, settled, perhaps even grounded by it. Plotinus says indeed that it is through the one that all the others have their appointed place (τόπος) (*Enn.* VI.9.6); indeed simply having an appointed place intensifies the differentiation from the one, which, spacing all things, is itself everywhere and nowhere.

By being differentiated from all things, the one is differentiated also from being, for, says Plotinus, "being is all things [τὸ γὰρ ὄν τὰ πάντα]" (*Enn.* VI.9.2). Reinscribing the phrase from the *Republic*, Plotinus will write again and again that the one is beyond being (ἐπέκεινα ὄντος).

The one is also differentiated specifically from the intellect: "It cannot be intellect, for in this way it would be all things, since intellect is all things" (*Enn.* VI.9.2). In knowing all things through their intelligible forms, intellect is as manifold as those forms; even if the forms were not many, the intellect would still, by its very nature, be coupled with the intelligible so as to be, at once, two, that is, not simply one (*Enn.* III.8.9). Even if, as with the best intellect, it does not look outside but turns to itself so as to become, at once, both that which thinks and that which is thought, still it will be double and not single, not the one. The one must be before the intellect, though its anteriority cannot be such as might be ascribed to that which would be known by the intellect, that is, the intelligible. For it belongs also to the nature of the intelligible to be coupled with the intellect, so that it is also, at once, two. The anteriority of the one is still more wonderful, and Plotinus writes of "this wonder of the one, which is not being [θαῦμα τοῦ ἕν, ὅ μὴ ὄν ἐστιν], so that 'one' may not here also have to be predicated of something else, which in truth has no fitting name, but if we must give it a name, 'one' would be an appropriate ordinary way of speaking of it, but not in the sense of something else and then one" (*Enn.* VI.9.5). It is not *one thing*, not *one being*. If it were at all, one would have to say simply that it is one. But it is not being, so that in saying that it is one, it is necessary to cross out the *is* of the *is one*. Even then, it will still be necessary to forgo the supposition that *one* is a fitting name for what would here be named. Little wonder that Plotinus concludes that to know it is difficult (χαλεπόν).[8]

Because it is apart from intellect and the intelligible, the one is differentiated also from everything that thinks and knows. Referring to the one, Plotinus writes: "No thinking, lest there be otherness [οὐδὲ νόησις, ἵνα μὴ ἑτερότης]." Even to think itself would require doubling and otherness; whereas the one, in its utterly self-sufficient union with itself "does not need thought of itself" (*Enn.* VI.9.6).

Thus is the one separated from all things, from being, from intellect and intelligible, from thinking and knowing, even from the *is* of the *is separated*, even from separation itself, even from the name *one* considered as a fitting name. To the one there pertains nothing that would violate its oneness, not even a fitting name, which, fitted to it, would then broach the duality of name and named. To the one there pertains nothing that would broach in it the slightest otherness, and it is this absolute exclusion of otherness, this utter absolution from alterity, that sets what is called the one utterly apart, that renders it absolutely other than all these other things, other than all things whatsoever. Its having within it no alterity whatsoever is precisely—if almost paradoxically—what gives the one itself its utter, its absolute alterity.

Plotinus never ceases to underline this alterity constituted through the absolute exclusion of alterity. The one is above all things (ὑπὲρ πάντα), and its hyperposition is necessary in order for it to be the ἀρχή of all things: "The all could not any more come into being if the origin did not remain by itself, other [ἐφ' ἑαυτῆς ἑτέρας]" (*Enn.* III.8.10). Even though all others remain around it (περὶ αὐτό), the one is not around any of them (*Enn.* III.9.9). Even in bringing it about that all beings are beings, the one remains always turned to itself.

Everything comes back to the spacing of the one by which, as it originates all things, being everywhere, it is also, at once, absolutely other than all things, utterly alone and apart in completely undisturbed

---

8. There is a resonance here with the *Timaeus* where, especially in the discourse on the third kind, the word χαλεπόν recurs in connections that are decisive for this discourse. See, for instance, *Tim*. 49b.

union with itself, slipping away even from discourse, which cannot but broach a doubling, even in the single word *one*, to say nothing of phrases like *union with itself*. One will want to ask: How is it that the one can be utterly apart and yet can originate all things? How can it be both separate and origin, considering that its originating of things does not qualify or limit its separateness, nor conversely? How, being nowhere, can it also be everywhere? Schürmann underscores the weight of this question: "Only one question haunts Plotinus: 'How did the One not remain in itself?'" (*HB*, 184). In other words, how, being in itself, did the one also give rise to all things?

The question is compounded—but also, it seems, sharpened—if it is also taken into account that each and every thing brought forth is itself one. Plotinus asks rhetorically: "For what could anything be if it was not one?" (*Enn.* VI.9.1). Each thing, then, to the degree that it *is*, is to that same degree one. This holds for all of the things originating from the one, whether they be intelligible or sensible. The same could be said of the good in the *Republic*: that it fathers images of itself (*Rep.* 506e). And, in both cases, asking about the mother, about her identity or at least her name, comes to more than merely following up on a perhaps imperfect analogy.

The question can now be posed more sharply: How can the one remain absolutely one, undergoing no doubling whatsoever, not even that of union with itself, *and yet* originate things that are themselves ones, things that are ones precisely to the degree that they are, that is, have been originated? But whatever is to a degree one can appropriately be called an image of the one. The question is thus: How can the one remain one while also fathering images of itself, many ones?

This is the point at which recourse to a Platonic text becomes decisive for the reading, specifically to a passage of the *Timaeus* that, despite the massive appropriation of this text from Aristotle on, remained fundamentally ineffective. I refer to the discourse on the χώρα; broached near the center of the *Timaeus*, its interpretation requires the most painstaking elaboration of its context if one is to avoid assimilating it to more familiar discourses and simply repeating the disabling that it underwent in ancient Platonism. Since that context has been elaborated elsewhere,[9] consideration will be given here only to the chorology itself (*Tim.* 52b–d).

9. *Chorology*, especially chapter 3.

In the passage it is a matter of maintaining the oneness of the one, its integrity, as it were, even in the instance in which, as with the Platonic εἴδη, there proves to be a pluralizing of the one, each intelligible εἶδος being itself one. What is to be maintained is the following, said in what Timaeus calls a precise true λόγος: "that as long as one thing is something and another is something else, neither of the two will ever come to be in the other, so as to become, at once [ἅμα], one (and the same) and two." The question is how to maintain this integrity of what is one while still allowing that images of it can be, that is, without consigning them to being nothing at all. Let me cite another part of the passage in which again what is said is said to be the truth: "for an image, since not even that itself on the basis of which it comes to be generated belongs to the image but it is always brought forth as the phantom [φάντασμα] of something other [ἕτερον]—." Let me interrupt for a moment in order to underline the bearing of what Timaeus is here saying: an image, for example, an image of the one, is a mere phantom of the original, which is other than the image and, especially in the case of the one, is absolutely other, that is, does not at all belong to the image, could not belong to the image without doubling itself, ceasing to be one, becoming, as Timaeus says, at once one and two. Timaeus continues: "because of this it is appropriate for it [the image] to be generated in something other, clinging to being at least in a certain way, on pain of being nothing at all." This other would be other than the image; it would also be other than the absolutely other, other than the one; thus it would constitute a third kind, a kind that would complicate and skew the opposition between the intelligible and the sensible. This other, this third kind, to which the image clings, or rather by which it is enabled to cling to being—this is what, prior to this most decisive passage, Timaeus has called *mother, nurse, receptacle*. Finally, in this passage he calls it χώρα. In lieu of a translation (*lieu* is a common translation), let it suffice to mention that what has been called *spacing* is meant to evoke something like (there is of course nothing like it, not even the nothing itself) what is called the χώρα.

How could the one remain in itself, lonely and apart, while also originating the many other ones that make up the whole of what is? Reinscribing the Platonic chorology within the opening of this question, one could say: this is possible only insofar as these ones originate in something like the χώρα. I say: *something like* the χώρα—not in order to suggest some positive similarity, some form had in common with the χώρα, for nothing could be similar to the χώρα in this sense, the χώρα having neither sense nor form. In proposing to reinscribe within Plotinian thought something like the χώρα, my intention with this phrase is primarily to forestall reducing the third kind to mere place in the visible cosmos. One could also say: spacing of the one—though now the genitive would become more complex than might have been supposed. Not only an objective genitive: the spacing of the one in the sense of its separation, its being set utterly apart from all beings. And not only, in addition, subjective genitive: the spacing by which the one originates all things, making them all in its image, as ones. But also, through the reinscription of the Platonic chorology, a spacing effected neither upon the one nor by the one; rather, a spacing that would first let these spacings take place together. A maternal spacing perhaps. In any case, the spacing that would make it possible for the one to be everywhere and nowhere.

Even aside from the recoil, as it were, of the one upon the discourse that would say it, its slipping away so as to require that the discourse be to an extent crossed out—even aside from this, there is still the question of vision, of a vision that would inhabit such discourse and give it its force. Such vision would finally have to come to the aid of the entire discourse on the spacings of the one. But if the one is set apart, absolutely other even than soul and intellect, how is vision of it possible? How can the one be seen, beheld, contemplated? How can it be brought within the sphere of vision without ceasing to be itself? How can the sphere of vision be extended up to the one if it is indeed absolutely other? And how can it be seen without that very vision bringing to bear upon it a doubling that would violate its inviolable oneness? How, then, is vision of the one possible? To say nothing of the possibility of a discourse that would attempt to match such vision, to double it by saying it.

Though the one is everywhere, it is not somewhere where one could cast one's vision upon it. Plotinus constantly insists that one will not be able to contemplate the one by casting one's vision outward, that instead one must turn within (πρὸς τὸ εἴσω). And yet, this turn is not a reversion to inner vision; it does not issue in self-knowledge. Plotinus says that, making the turn, one ignores oneself and comes instead to a vision of the one (see *Enn.* VI.9.7). But in this case how is it that one must turn inward? How is it that the turn inward can lead to a vision of the one? What does the turn inward accomplish?

The most telling indication of the character of the turn is provided by Plotinus' statement that on the way to vision of the one the soul must become formless (ἀνείδεον). This entails the abandonment of self-knowledge, since a soul without form could not be submitted to knowing, which would proceed precisely by way of form. Yet still, how does the soul's becoming formless serve to bring it onto the way to vision of the one?

This is another juncture at which a reinscription of Platonic chorology within Plotinian thought can be productive. For, in becoming formless, the soul would come to imitate the χώρα, which itself is utterly devoid of form, that is, is neither form nor informed as such. Becoming formless, the soul would become something like the χώρα, indeed in the only possible way. The soul would thus prepare to receive into itself something like an image of the one that would leave still intact the integrity, the utter separation, of the one. In other words, there would be prepared within the soul a spacing by which it would be with the one even though, on pain of there being two, it cannot be with the one.

Vision of the one requires a certain loss of self, becoming formless. It is, says Plotinus, as if one became other than oneself: in the vision of the one, one is not oneself, not a seer that would come to double the seen, making the one two. In the vision, one is not *one's own* (see *Enn.* VI.9.10). It is as if one were carried away in quiet solitude: a vision that exceeds vision, ἔκστασις (*Enn.* VI.9.11).

Yet it is not exactly an image of the one that is had in the vision. Later indeed, putting memory into play, remembering what one became—or rather, it would seem, construing it as a *what*—then one will have something like an image of it in oneself (see *Enn.* VI.9.11). Or, at least, if the possibility of the vision has to be explained to someone, it can be said that it occurs by way of the likeness (ὁμοίον) in oneself (*Enn.* III.8.9). But the proper name that Plotinus gives to this impropriety is neither image nor likeness but rather *trace* (ἴχνος), announcing the absolutely other without presenting and thus doubling it.[10]

10. In this connection Derrida refers to "the *trace* (*ikhnos*) of a certain nonpresence." This reference comes in a note in *Marges de la philosophie* (Paris: Les Éditions de Minuit, 1972), 206. The same note provides the epigraph for Reiner Schürmann's paper "Neoplatonic Henology as an Overcoming of Metaphysics": "The closure of metaphysics, which some audacities in the *Enneads* seem to indicate by transgressing it . . . ."

If now, finally, one turns back to Plato's *Republic*, to its center, to the account of the soul's ascent out of the cave upward toward the highest one, the sun, one cannot but wonder at the words with which Socrates tells Glaucon of the final stage of that ascent. At that stage one would no longer merely see its phantoms reflected in water or in other foreign places. Rather, in the final moment of vision one would come to behold it, as Socrates says, "by itself in its own χώρα" (*Rep.* 516b).

It is as in the choral dance that Plotinus describes (*Enn.* VI.9.8): when we look to the one in its singularity, alone and apart, when we look to it as to a conductor, we members of the chorus cease singing out of tune. Then, when we turn toward it, we sing beautifully and, in Plotinus' words, "we truly dance our god-inspired dance around it." Reiner Schürmann never ceased to show how fraught with aporias such turning and such seeing are. But he did nonetheless—in Greek fashion, in thinking—somehow teach us to sing and dance.

CHAPTER 5

GROUNDERS OF THE ABYSS

IT IS ALMOST THE SAME as with *Being and Time*, which, opening with a citation from Plato's *Sophist*, is cast as a renewal of the γιγαντομαχία περὶ τῆς οὐσίας. As *Being and Time* ventured to take up again the long since forgotten Platonic question of being, so does *Contributions to Philosophy* propose to take up again the Platonic beginning—Heidegger's Platonism, one might call it, or as he calls it, the first beginning. Even if the first beginning exceeds the Platonic texts in various ways, what Heidegger draws from those texts, his Platonism in this sense, forms its center; for it is around the determination of being as ἰδέα that everything openly belonging to the first beginning revolves.

But whereas, at least by certain of Heidegger's self-interpretations, *Being and Time* takes up the Platonic beginning in order to radicalize it and bring it to completion, *Contributions to Philosophy* is engaged in crossing to another beginning. Precisely for this reason it is the text in which a certain Platonic legacy reaches its highest pitch. It is cast beyond the completion of metaphysics, beyond the completion to which the Platonic beginning is brought by Hegel and by Nietzsche, even beyond the completion ventured by *Being and Time*. With *Contributions to Philosophy* it is as if a Platonic legacy were made to sound forth in a swan song. It is an intense, if mournful, song, and in it something previously unsung is made audible, something that silently enabled the circulation between ἰδέα and beings that Platonism celebrated. It is a song that one may, on the other hand, want to hear along with another swan song, the one sung by Socrates on his last day.

▼ ● ◆

But how is one even to read or write about *Contributions to Philosophy*, much less transpose it as if into song? It is imperative not to disguise its utter strangeness. It is a work that at the very outset disclaims being a work, at least of the style heretofore. It declares, too, that all fundamental words have been used up and that the genuine relation to the word has been destroyed. What is to be said of a book the very title of which is deliberately made to exemplify this destitution of words, even if with the utmost irony, as if the blandest of covers had been mockingly wrapped around this text, which, in starkest contrast, does not shy away from the most unheard-of—and, indeed, courageous[1]—ventures, letting words slide toward the most extreme limit, toward the unsayable to which saying would always already have submitted? As in what is, though parenthesized and set as if it were merely a subtitle, nonetheless called the proper, suitable, appropriate title: *Vom Ereignis*. How is one to read and to write (even translating into another language, perhaps even simulating transposition into song) of and from what would be said in this word that Heidegger himself later declared untranslatable?[2] What is one to make—or not make—of a text that says—and says that it says—"always the same of the same" (*B*, §39), weaving its tautological threads always around the same pole or at least around the single axis secured by that pole? What of a text that, at the other extreme, yokes together words that to all appearances speak against one another, issuing in such apparent contradictions as "grounders of the abyss"? To say nothing of the way in which the text crosses back over itself, crossing out what, in the crossing toward the other beginning, it could not but have put forth.

1. Referring to the beginning as the always withdrawing origin, Heidegger writes: "This unused-up power of the closure of the richest possibilities of courage (of the attuned-knowing will to *Ereignis*) is the only rescue and attestation" [*Beiträge zur Philosophie (Vom Ereignis)* (Frankfurt a.M.: Vittorio Klostermann, 1989), §23]. Subsequent references will be indicated by *B*, followed by the section number.

2. Heidegger, *Identität und Differenz* (Pfullingen: Günther Neske, 1957), 29.

How is one to read this strange text otherwise than as Nietzsche once demanded of his readers: "slowly, deeply, looking cautiously back and forth, with reservations, with doors left open, with delicate fingers and eyes"?[3] How is one to write of *Contributions to Philosophy* otherwise than by trying to keep one's bearings alongside some short stretches of the "pathway which is first traced out by the crossing to the other beginning, into which Western thinking is now entering" (*B*, §23)?

▼ ● ◆

It is remarkable that grounding weighs so heavily in this thinking that would cross to the other beginning. For, in this crossing, grounding would be exceeded, as would be indeed the entire orbit within which grounding was heretofore possible and was determined as such in the first beginning. Yet it is precisely through—as a result of—this transgression that the need for another grounding is exposed and the necessity of rehabilitating grounding, even if exorbitantly, is put into play. Grounding comes to figure so prominently that the word, even if used up in the history of metaphysics, can entitle one of the major fugal moments of Heidegger's text. And, from its beginning, *Contributions to Philosophy* celebrates those who are called "grounders of the abyss."

The thinking inscribed in *Contributions to Philosophy* begins at the end of metaphysics, begins within that indefinitely extending end in order to break with it, out of it, for the sake of another beginning. *Metaphysics* designates "the whole history of philosophy up to now" (*B*, §258), that which began in the first beginning and which came to its end (in the double sense of completion and termination) in Nietzsche's inversion of Platonism. With the Nietzschean inversion of the defining opposition between intelligible and sensible—that is, when the "true world" finally becomes a fable—the final possibility of Platonism is realized and the entire store of such possibilities, played out in the history of metaphysics, is exhausted (*B*, §91).[4]

---

3. Friedrich Nietzsche, *Morgenröthe*, in vol. V/1 of *Werke: Kritische Gesamtausgabe*, ed. Giorgio Colli and Mazzino Montinari (Berlin: Walter de Gruyter, 1971), 9.

4. See also Heidegger, *Nietzsche* (Pfullingen: Günther Neske, 1961), 1: 231–42.

What Nietzsche calls Platonism corresponds to what Heidegger calls the first beginning, though Heidegger's analysis goes well beyond any that Nietzsche ventured—except, in a very different register, in *The Birth of Tragedy*. According to Heidegger's analysis, the first beginning is marked by the eruption, among the Greeks, of the question regarding beings as a whole, regarding beings as such—the question as to what beings as such are, the question "What are beings?"[5]

Heidegger takes it to be a matter of necessity: in the arising of this question and thus in the first beginning as such, it is necessity that is operative. Yet, as pertaining to the first beginning, necessity does not have the sense determined for it in and by the first beginning. Heidegger's declaration of what is operative in the first beginning is itself already engaged in passing (*Zuspiel*) between this and another beginning. As thought in this passage, the necessity ascribed to the first beginning is not delimitable merely as one modal category alongside the other two, possibility and actuality. Rather, in the passing between beginnings, the necessary (*notwendig*) comes to be redetermined—says Heidegger—as a turning (*Wende*) out of a compelling need or distress (*nötigende Not*), a turning from need/distress and a turning compelled by need/distress. As that which is compelling in necessity, *Not* (perhaps best translated with the hendiadys need/distress) does not refer merely to misery and lack. Heidegger stresses that, though it may seem only negative, it is indeed something more originary, something that escapes the mere opposition between positive and negative. In the lecture course *Basic Questions of Philosophy*, which is contemporaneous with the composition of *Contributions to Philosophy*, Heidegger even says, of the need/distress that compels the first beginning, that "it is not a lack and not a deprivation but is the surplus of a gift, which, however, is more difficult to bear than any loss."[6] One would presume that it is difficult to bear precisely because of that to which, if one were to bear it, one would be compelled by it.

But what is the need/distress operative in the first beginning? In the lecture course Heidegger describes it as: "not knowing the way out

---

5. See Heidegger, *Vom Wesen der Wahrheit* in *Wegmarken*, vol. 9 of *Gesamtausgabe* (Frankfurt a.M.: Vittorio Klostermann, 1976), §4.

6. Heidegger, *Grundfragen der Philosophie: Ausgewählte "Probleme" der "Logik,"* vol. 45 of *Gesamtausgabe* (Frankfurt a.M.: Vittorio Klostermann, 1984), 153.

or the way in: out of and into that which such knowing first opens up as an unentered and ungrounded 'space.'" He calls this space first opened up by such knowing/not-knowing the "between," where, as he says, "it has not yet been determined what being [*seiend*] is or what non-being is, though where also there is not such total confusion and undifferentiation of beings and non-beings [*des Seienden und Unseienden*] as would sweep everything away and into everything else."[7] Set forth needfully/distressfully into this "between," the human being (*Mensch*) has for the first time the experience of finding himself in the midst of beings (*das Inmitten des Seienden*). Yet the very knowing that opens up the "between" and sets the human being forth in the midst of beings is haunted—says Heidegger—by not-knowing,[8] and it is precisely this not-knowing that constitutes the particular form of need/distress that holds sway in this opening. The need/distress breaks up beings so as to ground a possible standpoint for human being within this space; that is, it compels a casting asunder of what will be determined as beings in their being over against non-beings. Thus this need/distress provides to thinking in the first beginning its essential space, a space in which beings can come forth in their being and can thus be apprehended and named in their being for the first time. It is, then, this need/distress that attunes humans to beings in their being. Heidegger identifies this attunement with what the Greeks called θαυμάζειν (wonder) and identified as the origin of philosophy.

In the contemporaneous lecture course Heidegger goes on to indicate how from such attunement the first beginning came to issue in a determination of the being of beings. From within the passage (*Zuspiel*) between beginnings, it can be shown that an understanding of being as constant presence (*beständige Anwesenheit*) thoroughly guided this determination; indeed this insight, that the Greek determination of being was secretly guided by reference to a mode of time, was—as is well known—decisive for Heidegger in opening the way to

7. Ibid., 152.

8. Heidegger elaborates the not-knowing that constitutes the need/distress. He refers to "the open 'between' in which beings and non-beings stand forth as a whole, though still in their undifferentiatedness" and then continues: "Since the between is the *whole* of these undifferentiated beings, there is nothing outside to which an exit would be possible. And because it is a whole that is undifferentiated, there is nothing inside to which a way might lead as to a standpoint" (ibid., 160).

Being and Time and beyond. But in the first beginning as such, it was a matter of determining that which constitutes an answer to the question "What are beings as such?" It was a matter of determining their beingness (*Seiendheit*—Heidegger's translation of οὐσία), their whatness. The determination proceeded as follows: the beingness or whatness of a being consists in the look that is always presented by such a being, the look that indeed is sighted in advance and that thus enables the very recognition of any being as the being it is, the look that precedes the generation of any and every being that looks thus and survives the destruction of every such being. But the look—that is, what is seen when one sets out to see (ἰδεῖν) something—is the ἰδέα. Thus is being determined in the first beginning as the beingness of beings, and beingness, in turn, as ἰδέα.[9]

As the first beginning is carried through—and ever thereafter in the history of metaphysics—philosophy thinks the circulation between beingness and beings, reenacting the circling that is continually under way in the circuit linking beings to their beingness and beingness to those beings whose beingness it constitutes. This circulation is generated, on the one side, by the requirement that the ἰδέα be sighted in advance of beings and, on the other side, by the capacity of beings to present their ἰδέα. This is the circulation that is itself presented in the Platonic images of line and cave and even more conspicuously as such in the discussion, in the *Phaedo*, of the relation between remembrance and perception, between remembering what equality is and perceiving that certain things are equal. It is the circulation that, according to *Contributions to Philosophy*, is meant in the very name *metaphysics*: "The name is meant to say that thinking of being takes beings in the sense of what is present and extant as its starting point and goal for ascending to being, an ascending which immediately and at once turns again into a descending into beings" (*B*, §258). Thus metaphysics circles. Thus it circles in the circle originally traced in the Platonic texts. Thus it circles through all possible configurations of its circle, through what for Heidegger is the legacy of Platonism, until, with Nietzsche, it comes to its end. To the extent that ground and grounding are determined purely in reference to the circling between beings and beingness—as indeed they have been hereto-

9. See ibid., 60–71.

fore—the end of metaphysics is also the exhaustion of ground and grounding. The slightest move beyond, the merest gesture toward twisting free of the final—and thus of every—possibility of Platonism, cannot but disturb, indeed interrupt, ground as such. From the moment when, after the "true world" has finally become a fable, the abolition even of the apparent world is declared, and so, too, the abolition of the very opposition constitutive of Platonism and even of its inversion—from this moment one cannot but be exposed to an abyss.

Crossing to another beginning would bring, then, an overcoming of metaphysics, a leap beyond the first beginning and everything possible within its orbit. And yet, Heidegger insists that it is only in the crossing to another beginning that an originary appropriation of metaphysics and of its history becomes possible; that is, it is precisely at the point of its overcoming that metaphysics "first becomes recognizable in its essence" (*B*, §85).[10] What does it mean to recognize metaphysics in its essence? In a provisional formulation (which will itself eventually have to be twisted free),[11] one can say that it means: thinking and saying that which, in play in the first beginning as the very condition of its possibility, nonetheless went unthought and unsaid both in the first beginning and also, consequently, in the history of metaphysics. The unthought of the first beginning could, then, be said—provisionally—in a discourse on that by which the opening and

---

10. Here and throughout I have retained the traditional translation of *Wesen* as *essence*. While the two words do not have identical significations, both have served in the history of modern philosophy to translate the Latin *essentia*. While no one will dispute the fact that in *Contributions to Philosophy* the word *Wesen* comes to have a sense that diverges radically from that of *essentia*, it is, on the other hand, a major accomplishment of Heidegger's text to inscribe this common (and philosophically traditional) German word in a discourse so originary as to transform the sense of the word. To try to build that transformation into the very translation cannot but obscure it. For *Wesung*, which is not a common German word, I use the uncommon form *essency*, which was still current in seventeenth-century English.

11. This formulation, though for other reasons provisional, already engages the successively more originary redeterminations to which Heidegger submits essence in *On the Essence of Truth*. A marginal note by Heidegger makes explicit the succession of senses already virtually manifest in the text itself: "Essence: (1) *quidditas*—the 'what'—κοινόν; (2) enabling—condition of possibility; (3) ground of enabling" (*Vom Wesen der Wahrheit*, 177). Not only is essence thus linked to ground at an entirely new level (that of freedom as the essence/ground of truth) but also even essence as ground is referred to a still "more originary essence" at a level at which the determinations of essence and of truth converge.

sustaining of the difference between beings and their beingness becomes possible. In the same mode, one could say of this unthought that it is the condition that makes possible the circulation between beings and beingness, that enables the circling played out in the history of metaphysics. In the first beginning, philosophy would have passed over this condition—that is, the condition would have remained concealed precisely as it, at once, made possible everything that philosophy ventured in the first beginning. It is this unthought, unsaid condition, this "domain . . . completely hidden up to now" (*B*, unnumbered opening section) that would be thought and said in the crossing to another beginning ventured in *Contributions to Philosophy*.

One of the names that Heidegger proposes for this unthought of the first beginning—provisionally characterized as condition of possibility—is *Seyn* (*beyng*). The archaic spelling serves not only to distinguish it from *Sein als Seiendheit* (being as beingness) but also to suggest a certain anteriority with respect to the metaphysical concept of being.[12] As condition of possibility, as that by which the very space of the circulation between beings and beingness is first opened, beyng can itself be identified neither as a being nor as the beingness (whatness, ἰδέα) of beings.

Contributions to Philosophy ventures to say thoughtfully this unthought and unsaid condition of the very space of the first beginning, saying it, first of all, as beyng. Heidegger is acutely aware that such saying will have to strategize between two impossibilities: on the one side, the impossibility of saying beyng "with the ordinary language that today is ever more widely misused and destroyed by incessant talking" and, on the other side, the impossibility of inventing "a new language for beyng." Whereas in the first beginning the language of beings had an appropriateness, as philosophy addressed beings in their beingness, now, in crossing to another beginning, now, with the turn from the exhausted circuit of beings and beingness back to beyng, now, with this leap to beyng, which is neither a being nor the beingness of a being, one will, as Heidegger says, have "to say the language of beings as the language of beyng" (*B*, §36). The impossibility even of

12. Since the archaic character of the spelling is significant, it is preferable to translate *Seyn* as *beyng*, a form that was extant in English at least as late as the fourteenth century, rather than with the hyphenized *be-ing*.

the question "What is beyng?"—as if one could assume that beyng *is* and could ask about its whatness, its beingness—is indicative of the disruptive force of the turn. The only possibility will be some such strategy as the following: to grant within certain limits the everyday understanding of language as referring to beings and to "go a certain stretch of the way with it—in order then at the right moment to exact a turning in thinking" (*B*, §41). Whatever the strategy, the saying will remain precarious.

In *Contributions to Philosophy* Heidegger ventures to think and say the unthought of the first beginning in at least four ways. The first way is simply as *beyng*, the archaic spelling signaling the turn back to what can be called—provisionally—an anterior condition. The second way says the same but says it as the *essence of beyng*. Heidegger is explicit that, in this phrase, *essence* (as essency [*Wesung*]) "does not name something that yet again lies *beyond* beyng" (*B*, §164). Again: it "is never a way of beyng that is added on to beyng or even one which persists in itself above beyng" (*B*, §166). Displaced from such senses as κοινόν and γένος, essence adds nothing to beyng, and *the essence of beyng* says the same as *beyng* itself. What the tautological inscription is to mark is only that beyng holds sway (*west*) as happening (*Geschehnis*).[13] Beyng is—to say it improperly—nothing other than its happening, and the essence of beyng is, as Heidegger expands the saying, the "happening of the truth of beyng" (*B*, §166). It goes without saying that everything will depend on properly determining the sense of happening; this determination, differentiating the happening of beyng from mere ontic occurrences, will lead directly into a renewal of the question of grounding, a renewal that, putting into play the old, used-up word, will attempt at the right moment to exact a turning in thinking.

The third way says the unthought of the first beginning as the truth of beyng. Heidegger observes that this expression does not mean the truth about beyng, as if it referred to one or several correct assertions about beyng that could be so entitled and taken to constitute a

13. Thus, near the end of *On the Essence of Truth*, at a point where the full displacement of the sense of *essence* has been accomplished, Heidegger says that *essence* is to be understood verbally (*verbal*), even though, still remaining at this point within metaphysical representation, thinking identifies essence "as the difference holding sway between being and beings [*als den waltenden Unterschied von Sein und Seiendem*]" (*Vom Wesen der Wahrheit*, 201).

doctrine or theory about beyng. Heidegger observes also that the expression does not mean true beyng in the sense of beyng that is actual, as if beyng were not anterior to beings and to such modes as actuality. He says, rather: "This truth of beyng is nothing at all different from beyng, but rather its ownmost essence [*Diese Wahrheit des Seyns ist gar nichts vom Seyn Verschiedenes, sondern sein eigenstes Wesen*]" (*B*, §44). The tautology is explicit: the truth of beyng is beyng (which) is the essence of beyng. But what the expression *the truth of beyng* accentuates is the character of beyng as ἀλήθεια, as the clearing/concealment in and through which beings come to show themselves in their being. In this expression the character of beyng as condition of possibility is—if still provisional—most prominent. Heidegger indicates this as follows: For truth "is the between [*das Zwischen*] for the essency [*Wesung*] of being and the beingness of beings. This between grounds the beingness of beings in beyng" (*B*, §5). The point is not that the truth of beyng, because it is between the essence of beyng and the beingness of beings, is therefore something other than, something apart from, the essence of beyng. The point is, rather, that it is as truth, as clearing/concealment, that beyng happens in such a way that beings can come to present themselves in their beingness. Around precisely this point Heidegger broaches the concept of another ground, assuming that, within the orbit of this other ground, one could continue to speak of concept. No longer identified with the beingness of beings, this other ground—the between, the truth of beyng—would ground the beingness of beings. One could call it a kind of ground of ground, a ground before ground—though only as long as one kept intact the metaphysical circuit and held back from the leap beyond its end. Outside and beyond, the very determination of the being (of beings) as beingness would erode in such a way as to prepare a transmutation of being itself.

In the fourth way of saying the unthought of the first beginning, the requirement of ground and grounding is decisive. Yet in this connection what is required is not just the grounding of beingness on (the truth of) beyng as its ground; rather, what must be grounded is the truth of beyng itself. Heidegger writes "that the essency of beyng requires the grounding of the *truth* of beyng and that this grounding must be enacted as *Da-sein*" (*B*, §88). Under the requirement that it be grounded, the truth of beyng— beyng in its very happening—makes its own those who are capable of such grounding; it appropriates those who, precisely by enacting Da-sein, can ground the truth of beyng. As appropriating those needed, beyng happens—and this is the fourth way of saying it—as Ereignis.[14] But how is it that grounding is enacted as Da-sein? How is it that, in Heidegger's stark formulation, "Da-sein is the grounding of the truth of beyng" (*B*, §83)? What kind of grounding can Da-sein provide? What kind of ground can Da-sein be? What is Da-sein?—to risk a question that crosses back over itself, putting in question the very appropriateness of the *what* (that is, of *whatness*) to that which is called Da-sein. These questions touch on the heart of the thinking and discourse of grounding.

"Beyng holds sway [*west*] as Ereignis" (*B*, §10): this is what is said—from a distinctive essential domain—in each of the fugal moments of *Contributions to Philosophy*; this is what is said in saying always the same of the same. Always it is said of beyng that it happens as Ereignis. Always it is said of beyng and of the essence of beyng and of the truth of beyng—for these are the same—that they happen as Ereignis.

In thus saying always the same of the same, *Contributions to Philosophy* would say the unthought of the first beginning. Yet Heidegger repeatedly underlines the difference between the question of beings, that is, the guiding-question belonging to the first beginning, and the question of beyng, that is, the grounding-question that was passed over in the first beginning but is now to become the question proper to the other beginning. In the first beginning, being is thought as the beingness of beings and hence within the purview of beings.[15] But, in the other beginning, being is not to be thought within this purview, not to be thought from beings: "Thus beyng can no longer be thought from beings; it must be thought from out of itself" (*B*, §2). Beyng is to be thought from out of itself, not from beings, *and yet* the truth of beyng requires a grounding. Heidegger writes in behalf of the "thoughtful saying" that has crossed over to the ground-question (*Grundfrage*) and that can thus be indicative of this grounding: "This thoughtful saying is a directive. It indicates the open sheltering of the truth of

---

14. Taking Heidegger at his word that *Ereignis* can no more be translated than can the Greek λόγος and the Chinese *Tao* (*Identität und Differenz*, 29), I have left it untranslated throughout, while, on the other hand, developing in the discourse around it its affinity with happening and with appropriation.

15. ". . . from the very beginning being as beingness is experienced and thought *only* in terms of 'beings'—from beings, so to speak, from *and* back to the manifold" (*B*, §110).

beyng in beings as a necessity, without being a command" (*B*, §2). Here, then, it is a matter of necessity, of turning out of need/distress: grounding the truth of beyng must involve sheltering the truth of beyng in beings, sheltering it in beings that are, on the other hand, themselves in the open, hence, in precisely this sense—conjoining apparent opposites—an open sheltering (*Freie der Bergung*). Yet, in turn, the determination of grounding through this conjunction belongs to a larger configuration in which is expressed one of the major tensions running through *Contributions to Philosophy*: on the one hand, the truth of beyng must be thought from itself and not (as in the first beginning) from beings; but, on the other hand, the truth of beyng must be sheltered in beings and to this extent still thought—if differently—within a certain purview of beings. Yet the difference is all-decisive: the truth of beyng is to be brought to an *open* sheltering in beings, to a sheltering in beings that not only are in the open but that, precisely by sheltering the truth of beyng, open up that very expanse.

▼ ● ◆

Contributions to Philosophy sketches a double movement with respect to the first beginning: crossing to the other beginning would be, at the same time, going back into the first beginning, going back through the first beginning to the originary essence that remained concealed in the first beginning and throughout its entire course as metaphysics. This double movement, this passing (*Zuspiel*) between beginnings, is what is carried out in pursuing the question "What is metaphysics?"—the *what* designating here, not the whatness of a finally defined concept of metaphysics, but rather the concealed ground of metaphysics, the ground concealed so essentially that the concealment belonged to the very constitution of metaphysics. Thus it is that going back into the ground of metaphysics "is already no longer metaphysics but rather its overcoming" (*B*, §85).

It is also a double movement with respect to the Platonic legacy. On the one side, the movement is one of taking up that legacy in such a way as to be driven on beyond it, using its resources in order to overcome it. But, on the other side, the movement is one of inquiring back, not just into the source of the legacy, but into what was held back from the legacy that was passed along, into what precisely was not—and, Heidegger would say, could not have been—passed along.

But what about this concealed ground, which, provisionally, has been characterized as a condition of possibility, as that which makes possible the differentiation of beingness and beings and the circulation within the circuit of that difference? Did that which first made it possible for beings to be apprehended and named in their beingness remain utterly concealed in the first beginning? Was this making-possible, this enabling, simply, unknowingly assumed? Heidegger's own account in the contemporaneous lecture course would suggest otherwise: it is a knowing that first opens up the between, the *in the midst* of beings, where their determination in their beingness becomes possible. And what unfolds that possibility is the not-knowing, the need/distress, that haunts that knowing and that, in enabling the determination of beings, attunes the human being to beings in their being, gives him that attunement that the Greeks call θαυμάζειν. That such enabling did not remain concealed is evident not only in Heidegger's account of it but also from the Platonic texts themselves, which recognize and celebrate the way in which philosophy originates from wonder and from a certain not-knowing, that is, ignorance, that haunts knowing.

In what sense, then, is the happening of beyng the concealed ground operative in the first beginning? How is it the concealed ground if not as that which enables, if not as condition of possibility, if not as that which is prior to the determination of beings in their being, that is, as what came to be called the *a priori*? For Heidegger leaves no doubt but that the happening of beyng is not, in this sense, prior: "But beyng is not something 'earlier'—subsisting for and in itself. Rather, Ereignis is the temporal-spatial simultaneity of beyng and beings" (*B*, §5). Not that Heidegger denies that the regress to prior conditions has, within limits, its legitimacy: "Within beings and the interpretation of beings on the basis of their beingness in the sense of representedness (and already of ἰδέα), the regress to 'presuppositions' and 'conditions' makes sense and is right" (*B*, §44). Not that Heidegger denies even that such a way of thinking remains inevitable in the crossing to the other beginning: "Such a return, therefore, has become the basic form of 'metaphysical' thinking in manifold modifications, to such a degree that even the overcoming of 'metaphysics' toward an inceptual understanding cannot do without this way of thinking" (*B*, §44). And yet, if one cannot but go a stretch of this way—as indeed we have—one must also break with it, recognizing that the *a priori* is essentially connected to the ἰδέα and thus to beingness: "the *a priori* is really only there where ἰδέα is" (*B*, §112). In other words, to think being as *a priori* is ultimately to place it in the purview of beingness and beings and would be simply to repeat the obliteration of the difference. In the crossing to the other beginning, there must come a point at which one breaks decisively with thinking beyng as the *a priori*.

Beyond this point one will no longer, on the way to beyng, engage a regress that merely redoubles the metaphysical regress from beings to *a priori* beingness. If there should eventually prove to be a way in which beyng grounds beings so as to let them come forth in their being, that way will depend on—will be itself grounded by—the grounding of beyng itself. If, in this grounding, as Heidegger writes, "the ground grounds as a-byss" (*B*, §9),[16] then everything will hinge on the grounding—or grounders—of the abyss.

▼ ● ◆

Interrupting this development, taking some distance from it, we need to address a question that throughout the foregoing has become ever more pressing, even distressing certain moments of the development. Here, too, it is a matter of necessity, not just in the sense that Heidegger has let unfold, much less in the metaphysical sense of a modal category, but rather in the sense that the Greeks expressed in the word ἀνάγκη. As when, for instance, in the *Timaeus* a contrast is drawn between what comes about through νοῦς and what comes about through ἀνάγκη.[17]

The question concerns the ground of the circulation of being, concerns whether this obscure ground went unthought by the Greeks. More precisely: Did the obscure ground that makes possible—or in some more oblique fashion grounds—the circulation between beingness and beings remain concealed, utterly unthought, by the very thought—that presented in the dialogues—that traced this circulation in a decisive and inaugural way? Does one find in the Platonic dialogues only remote echoes of this ground, as in the celebration of θαυμάζειν

16. Instead of the neologism *abground* (and in view of Heidegger's own remark against inventing new language [*B*, §36]), *abyss* has been retained to translate *Abgrund*. Since *abyss* transliterates ἄβυσσος (α-privative + βύσσος [bottom]), it corresponds closely to *Abgrund* and allows etymologically the same hyphenization (*a-byss*) that Heidegger employs.

17. See *Chorology*, 91–93.

and in the recognition of the ignorance that haunts human knowledge? Or does the obscure ground not come to be thought—in its utter strangeness and its obscurity—at that point in the dialogues, most notably in the *Timaeus*, where the twofold of beingness and beings—Platonically expressed: of ἰδέα and image—comes to be put in question? This is the point where the circulation is interrupted or rather where its very possibility is shown to require a third kind, that which is most properly called (not without threatening propriety as such) the χώρα. As a third kind over against the ἰδέα, this condition has nothing to do with the *a priori*.

Is χώρα not, then, precisely the name under which the obscure condition came to be thought in the Platonic text? Is it not in the chorology that one finds, then, a Platonic counterpart to the movement back through the first beginning ventured in *Contributions to Philosophy*? To be sure, the chorology did not become part of the Platonic legacy; its reduction and effective exclusion is already at work as early as Aristotle.[18] The Platonic chorology is rather something held back from the legacy, something not passed along, except for the traces remaining in the text of the *Timaeus*. Yet those traces endure beyond that Platonism that chorology already exceeds; they reach beyond the reach of Platonism as metaphysics. It is, then, from the limit, from a Platonism at the limit of metaphysics, that this forgotten legacy can, as it were, be restored.

From this limit one might also hear—almost as in a dream—a song of this obscure condition, hear it sung in Socrates' swan song, especially in his song of the earth.

▼ ● ◆

For Heidegger everything hinges on the grounding—or grounders—of the abyss.

Heidegger writes of them almost at the very outset of *Contributions to Philosophy*, sketching in broad strokes what comes about with them: "At times those grounders of the abyss must be consumed in the fire of that which is safeguarded [*das Verwahrten*], so that Da-sein becomes possible for the human being [*dem Menschen*] and thus constancy [*Beständigkeit*] in the midst of beings is rescued, so that in the

18. See, above, chapter 2; also *Chorology*, chapter 5.

open of the strife between earth and world beings themselves undergo a restoration" (*B*, §2).

Who are the grounders of the abyss? Among them are those who question: "Those who question have set aside all curiosity; their seeking loves the abyss, in which they know the oldest ground" (*B*, §5).[19] For those who question, being grounders of the abyss does not mean installing a ground that would cancel the abyss as such but rather apprehending the abyss as archaic ground, as an abysmal ground older than beingness as ground. Yet, before all else, what these grounders ground is beyng in its truth; their accomplishment—indeed the accomplishment of all grounders of the abyss—is to ground the truth of beyng in this abysmal ground.

Those who question are not the only grounders of the abyss. Indeed, in what he says of them—that at times they must be consumed in the fire of that which is safeguarded—Heidegger's reference is primarily to the poet, to the poet of poets. For Hölderlin, in poetizing the essence of poetry, depicts the poet as exposed to the danger of being consumed by the fire of that which otherwise would go unbequeathed but which the poet can receive and hand down to the people. Cited and discussed in Heidegger's 1934–1935 lecture course on Hölderlin,[20] the lines come from "Wie wenn am Feiertage . . .":

> Und daher trinken himmlisches Feuer jezt
> Die Erdensöhne ohne Gefahr.
> Doch uns gebührt es, unter Gottes Gewittern,
> Ihr Dichter! mit entblösstem Haupte zu stehen
> Des Vaters Stral, ihn selbst, mit eigner Hand
> Zu fassen und dem Volk ins Lied
> Gehüllt die himmlische Gaabe zu reichen.

---

19. *Curiosity (Neugier)* designates in *Being and Time* the form that understanding takes in everydayness: "When curiosity has become free, its concern is to see, not in order to understand what it sees, that is, to come into a being toward it, but *only* in order to see. It seeks novelty only to leap from it again to another novelty" (*Sein und Zeit*, 172).

20. Heidegger, *Hölderlins Hymnen "Germanien" und "Der Rhein,"* vol. 39 of *Gesamtausgabe* (Frankfurt a.M.: Vittorio Klostermann, 1980), 30f. See also the 1939–1940 lecture devoted to this hymn, published as "Wie wenn am Feiertage . . ." in *Erläuterungen zu Hölderlins Dichtung*, vol. 4 of *Gesamtausgabe* (Frankfurt a.M.: Vittorio Klostermann, 1981).

In Hamburger's translation ("As on a Holiday . . ."):

> And hence it is that without danger now
> The sons of Earth drink heavenly fire.
> Yet, fellow poets, us it behoves to stand
> Bare-headed beneath God's thunderstorms,
> To grasp the Father's ray, no less, with our own two hands
> And, wrapping in song the heavenly gift,
> To offer it to the people.[21]

It is to the grounders of the abyss that Heidegger refers when he writes of the "*few individuals* . . . on the essential paths of grounding Da-sein [*des gründenden Da-seins*]," distinguishing them from "the random and resistless many who come later but who have nothing more before them and nothing more behind them" (*B*, §45). The allusions to Nietzsche, to *Thus Spoke Zarathustra*, could hardly be more transparent: set apart from the last men, those called grounders of the abyss and grounders of the truth of beyng are to *go under*, somewhat as Zarathustra went under so as to expose what underlies Platonism (and "Platonism for the people") and to bring about the going-under of man himself.[22] Those who go under are given over to what is to come (*B*, §250). These grounders of the abyss are the ones who come to something, to something beyond man as heretofore extant; they are the ones to whom something thus comes. They are the ones to come, those of the future (*die Zukünftigen*).

Whether exposing themselves to the consuming fire of heaven or erotically seeking in the abyss the oldest ground or going under so as to remain true to the earth, the grounders of the abyss do so in order that Da-sein become possible for humans (*Menschen*). It is a matter of enabling the human not just to be a being but to let there open a clearing in which beings can come to presence—perhaps even at the cost of the human being's becoming less a being (*unseiender*) (see *B*, §83). Thus would it become possible for the human "to be the

---

21. Friedrich Hölderlin, *Poems and Fragments*, trans. Michael Hamburger (Ann Arbor: University of Michigan Press, 1966), 375, 377.

22. See Heidegger's discussion of Zarathustra's *Untergang* in the 1937 lecture course *Nietzsches metaphysische Grundstellung im abendländischen Denken*, vol. 44 of *Gesamtausgabe* (Frankfurt a.M.: Vittorio Klostermann, 1986), §5.

Da as the ground needed by the essence of beyng" (*B*, §5). And thus would "constancy in the midst of beings" be rescued amidst the collapse of beingness, that is, of the constancy (constant presence) that was established through the yoke of the ἰδέα in the first beginning. And thus "in the open of the strife between earth and world beings themselves [are to] undergo a restoration." The task is "to restore beings from out of the truth of beyng" (*B*, §4): to restore to them, to be sure, something of what they have lost through the onslaught of machination, but in the only way possible in the other beginning, by letting them *be* within such happening of the truth of beyng as happens in the strife between earth and world.

And yet, Heidegger insists that a restoration of beings can come to pass only from out of a grounding of the truth of beyng. And, in turn, a grounding of the truth of beyng can come about, he insists, only from out of a leap, a daring, venturesome, dangerous leap by which everything familiar is abandoned. Indeed it is not just a matter of abandoning everything on which everyday life depends but of leaping away from all this; it is not just a matter of abstaining, as in adopting an ascetic stance, but of leaving everything behind in the most decisive and essential way: "The leap, the most daring move in the proceeding of inceptual thinking, abandons and casts behind itself [*wirft . . . hinter sich*] everything familiar, expecting nothing from beings immediately" (*B*, §115). Thus it is a matter of a leap away from beings as providing any immediate support, guidance, direction; more fundamentally, it is a leap away from beings as capable of providing any understanding of being, of supplying the sense either of their own being or of the being of that being that we ourselves are. The leap thus constitutes a break with, a decisive turn from, the determination of being within the purview of beings, the determination that determined the first beginning. Once one lets go entirely of beings, even the possibility of grounding being on beings dissolves, and one loses—even for oneself as being—all possibility of ground. Through the leap all grounds fall away, and one exposes oneself utterly to the abyss. The grounders *of the abyss* are such, first of all, in the sense that they are utterly exposed to the abyss and must endure being *in and of it*. To be sure, Heidegger declares that the leap releases also a certain belongingness to beyng: the grounders of the abyss are claimed, appropriated, for grounding the truth of beyng and are attuned (in awe) to this claim (see *B*, §115). Nonetheless, neither the claim nor the attunement gives them anything, as it were, to hold onto. Even as claimed and attuned, the grounders remain in the abyss, of the abyss; for it is only through their grounding the truth of beyng that a ground—though ever so precarious—is gained. The grounders are of the abyss in that, from within the abyss, they bring forth (through grounding) a ground within the abyss. From out of the abyss, their grounding is a "grounding of the abysmal ground" (*B*, §226).

▼ ● ◆

With the grounding question it is man's engagement that gets put to the question. In *Contributions to Philosophy* Heidegger continues to stress, as he had in the Marburg lectures, that, from the Greeks on, the development of the question of being had always followed the guiding thread provided by reference to such things as soul, reason, spirit, thinking, that is, by essential reference to the human being. But in these lectures what Heidegger brings out is the continuity with this recurrent reference to the human: "the ontology of Dasein represents the latent goal and constant and more or less evident demand of the whole development of Western philosophy."[23] In *Contributions to Philosophy*, on the other hand, what emerges is "that somehow the human being and yet again not the human being, namely, in an extension and a displacement, is in play in the grounding of the truth of beyng." Heidegger adds: "And it is precisely this question-worthy [matter] that I call Da-sein" (*B*, §193).

Beyng comes to truth only on the ground of Da-sein, only through the grounding brought by Da-sein (see *B*, §168). Da-sein is the ground of the truth of beyng, the ground through whose grounding beyng happens. Da-sein is not to be identified with the human being; its name is not to be taken as just an updated name for the being previously called human (*Mensch*). Da-sein is not something to be found in the extant human being, neither an inherent structure nor an emergent form nor an intrinsic capability; on the contrary, through the grounding brought by Da-sein, the grounding of the truth of beyng, "the human being is transformed from the ground up [*von Grund aus*]"

23. Heidegger, *Die Grundprobleme der Phänomenologie*, vol. 24 of *Gesamtausgabe* (Frankfurt a.M.: Vittorio Klostermann, 1975), 106.

(*B*, §170)—from out of this very ground and its grounding. Or, in another idiom, the human being as he was heretofore—"a rope over an abyss"—goes under.

Needed in order that beyng be brought to its truth, Da-sein is appropriated by beyng. Only in and through this appropriation does beyng happen at all. Its essential happening can, then, be called *Ereignis*, and, in English, this word will then need to be woven into a discourse charged by the significations of *ownness* (*making its own*, in the double sense), *appropriation*, and *happening*. The human being, too, while going under as he was heretofore, is, on the other side, also appropriated: "The Da is appropriated [*ereignet*] by beyng itself, and consequently the human being, as guardian of the truth of beyng, is appropriated and thus belongs to Da-sein in a distinctive and unique way" (*B*, §175). But how is it that the human being is the guardian of the truth of beyng? And how is the human being related to Da-sein such that he can come to belong to Da-sein in a distinctive, indeed unique way?

These questions can be addressed only if the question of Da-sein itself is first taken up. One would like to ask: What is Da-sein, if not simply the human being or some aspect of the extant human? Yet one can do so only to the extent that one frees the *what*, letting it metamorphize in the direction indicated by the displacement of essence in play in Heidegger's work from 1930 on.[24] Here is one answer to the question: Da-sein "is itself the being of the Da [*das Sein des Da*]." Heidegger continues: "The Da, however, is the openness of beings as such as a whole, the ground of more originarily thought ἀλήθεια." What the word *Da-sein* says is: *that there is a Da*—not just a determinable here and there (*hier und dort*) but, as Heidegger says, a "clearing [*Lichtung*] of beyng itself whose openness first spaces the space for every here and there." What the word *Da-sein* says is: *that a clearing opens*. Even further: Da-sein is "the essency of that opening which first opens up the self-concealing (the essence of beyng) and

24. That is, from the time of the initial version of "On the Essence of Truth." In this regard, one should note also Heidegger's insistence that *Da-sein* cannot be translated: "In *that* meaning which is for the first time and essentially introduced in *Being and Time* this word [*Da-sein*] cannot be translated, i.e., it resists the perspectives of previous ways of thinking and saying in Western history: *Da sein*" (*B*, §176).

which is thus the truth of beyng" (*B*, §173).[25] The grounding that Da-sein brings to the truth of beyng by the opening of a clearing for—within—the self-concealing of beyng itself is so essential to the happening of the truth of beyng that Heidegger lets *grounding* slide virtually into identity.

But what, then, of Da-sein and the human? On the one hand, the grounding is such as to require that the human being come to it (*B*, §130). This connection is also borne by the expression *menschliches Dasein*, in which, says Heidegger, the reference to the human indicates "the uniqueness of that being, the human, to whom alone Da-*sein* is proper" (*B*, §176). This connection—though not only it—leads Heidegger to say: "Beyng needs the human being in order that it hold sway [*wese*], and the human being belongs to beyng that he might accomplish his utmost vocation [*Bestimmung*] as Da-sein" (*B*, §133).

In another regard, the relation between Da-sein and the human being is said to lie in Da-sein's being the ground of the possibility of the human being's future (*des künftigen Menschseins*), that is, "the human being *is* futural insofar as he undertakes to be the Da" (*B*, §173). Otherwise he remains among the many who come along later but have nothing more before them and nothing more behind them—that is, he remains apart from the grounders of the abyss, apart even from those allied with them (see *B*, §45).

Da-sein is what both under-grounds the human and raises him to excess (*zugleich unter-gründet und überhöht*) (*B*, §176). Da-sein grounds the human but in a grounding in which the human, as he was hitherto, goes under. This under-grounding is precisely what is at issue in the declaration that Da-sein is both ground and abyss for historical humanity (see *B*, §194). Da-sein grounds the future human and buries the human as he has been. At the same time, the human is raised, elevated: belonging to beyng, the human (grounded by Da-sein) contributes to opening and preserving a clearing in the midst of concealment, a clearing within a concealment (the self-concealing withdrawal of beyng) that utterly exceeds all clearing. It seems that the human

25. ". . . grounding itself *clears* [lichtet] *the self-concealing* . . ." (*B*, §130). "The formulation 'Truth is, first of all, clearing concealment [*lichtende Verbergung*]' means: that a clearing is grounded for the self-concealing [*das Sichverbergende*]. The self-concealing of beyng in the clearing of the Da" (*B*, §217).

can come to be so engaged by this excess that he broaches an exceeding of himself as (a) being—in the sense thus outlined by Heidegger: "The less a being [*unseiender*] the human is and the less he insists upon the being [*das Seiende*] that he finds himself to be, so much nearer does he come to being [*Sein*]" (*B*, §83). Presumably it is thus that the human is *überhöht* by Da-sein—not just raised or elevated but raised to excess, elevated excessively.

But *how* is it that the human being comes to be grounded in Da-sein (and thus under-grounded and raised in excess)? How, in particular, is it that the grounders of the abyss come to be grounded by Da-sein, by that abysmal ground itself? Heidegger's answer is unequivocal: they come to be grounded in Da-sein precisely by becoming grounders of Da-sein; and this they do in and by creating (*B*, §195). But creating means: sheltering (*Bergen*) the truth of beyng in beings (*B*, §7). It is because the human being is the one by whom the truth of beyng comes to be sheltered in a being that the human can be the guardian of the truth of being.

Heidegger says: "The grounding of Da-sein happens as the sheltering of truth," its sheltering, through creating, in a being (*B*, §219). In a sense, everything pertinent to grounding is gathered in the phrase *the grounding of Da-sein*. At least three distinct senses are in play and in interplay. The phrase signifies (1) the grounding of the truth of beyng by Da-sein, that is, through the opening of a clearing for beyng; (2) the grounding (as under-grounding) of the human being by Da-sein (through which the human being comes to the opening and preserving of clearing); and (3) the grounding of Da-sein by the human being through the creating in which the truth of beyng comes to be sheltered in a being. The point is that these three groundings happen at once (ἅμα), and this *at once* is said in the word *Ereignis*. This is why in the passage (cited above) in which Heidegger sets beyng apart from the concept of the *a priori*, he says that "Ereignis is the temporal-spatial simultaneity of beyng and beings" (*B*, §5).

The human being becomes a grounder of the abyss—that is, of the abysmal ground Da-sein—by creating, by sheltering the truth of beyng in a being. For instance, in an artwork, which, in instigating the strife of earth and world, lets the truth of beyng happen. As with the temple at Paestum, which once opened and sustained a Greek world borne by the self-secluding earth. But it is of utmost significance that such sheltering is not something *nachträglich*: "Sheltering is not a subsequent housing [*das nachträgliche Unterbringen*] of an extant, subsistent truth within a being" (*B*, §243). Or, as Heidegger declares decisively in *The Origin of the Work of Art*: "But truth does not exist in itself beforehand, somewhere among the stars, only subsequently to descend elsewhere among beings . . . . Clearing of openness [i.e., the truth of beyng] and establishment in the open [i.e., being sheltered in a being such as an artwork] belong together. They are the same single essence of the happening of truth."[26] The opening of a clearing (grounding the truth of beyng) happens as the grounders of the abyss come, within the clearing, to shelter the truth of beyng in a being. Yet it is not as though there is first the truth of beyng, which then, subsequently, gets sheltered. From the point of view of the human, who has leaped into the abyss, it is not as though he somehow already—perhaps even always already—had the truth in view and then (keeping his gaze fixed on it, holding to it) could eventually shelter it, that is, express it or translate it. But if—letting the *is* slide toward *Ereignis*—one can say that there is no truth before it is sheltered, this does not mean, on the other hand, that the sheltering brings the truth of beyng about as a result; it is not as though there is creative sheltering and only then, subsequently, the truth of beyng. Rather, the truth of beyng and its sheltering happen *at once*. What is perhaps most demanding is to think this *at once*.

Heidegger declares that the truth of beyng can be sheltered in many ways: "in thinking, poetizing, building, leading, sacrificing, suffering, celebrating" (*B*, §177).[27]

Aside from—but also including—the distinctive beings in which truth is sheltered, beings are grounded in the truth of beyng; it is only from out of this grounding—and not through mere explanatory derivation from other beings—that beings can be known (*B*, §118). Yet this grounding of beings as such occurs only within the opening and sheltering accomplished in the grounding of Da-sein. Thus Heidegger says that beyng "holds sway [*west*] *before* all beings that stand within

26. Heidegger, *Der Ursprung des Kunstwerkes*, in *Holzwege*, vol. 5 of *Gesamtausgabe* (Frankfurt a.M.: Vittorio Klostermann, 1977), 49. This work was first presented as lectures in 1935–1936.

27. Another enumeration suggests an even broader range: "tool-preparation [*Zeuganfertigung*], machination-arrangement (technicity), creating works, deeds that establish states, thoughtful sacrifice" (*B*, §32). See also the enumeration in *The Origin of the Work of Art* (*Ursprung des Kunstwerkes*, 49).

it, something that of course can never be grasped according to the hitherto '*a priori*'" (*B*, §180).

Neither can Da-sein as ground (of the truth of beyng and, mediately, of beings as such) be grasped according to the concept of ground that identifies ground with the constant presence constituted as beingness in the first beginning. Heidegger marks this differentiation by saying with regard to the grounding of Da-sein that "the ground grounds as a-byss" (*B*, §9); he calls this grounding a "grounding of the abysmal ground" (*B*, §226). Heidegger links the abysmality of Da-sein to being-toward-death (see *B*, §163) but also—and in the end there is perhaps no difference—to the character of Da-sein as time-space. The utter differentiation from the concept of ground as nonspatial, eternal beingness goes without saying as Heidegger displaces ground (as Da-sein) into a displaced time-space: "Da-sein is to be taken as time-space, not in the sense of the usual concepts of time and space but as the momentary site [*Augenblicksstätte*] for the grounding of the truth of beyng" (*B*, §200). At such a momentary site ground will always be also abyss, the retreat of ground.

Thus will the few who take up the grounding of Da-sein be grounders of the abyss. Precisely as they ground and shelter the unspeakable excess of the utterly strange truth of beyng. In going under, while standing, aloof, courageously reaching for the heavenly fire.

CHAPTER 6

URANIC TIME

THERE ARE THINGS THAT LET one almost see light itself.

At certain moments. At moments quite incalculable. At moments indeed unforeseeable until a certain quiet receptiveness comes over one's vision, descending upon it as the gift of opening.

Then a kind of reversal is, if not actually effected, simulated almost to the point of actualization: a reversal in which one would come to see that which, while making vision possible, while giving it its very sense, remains itself invisible. For ordinarily one sees merely things, things illuminated, but not the light itself that comes to illuminate them. Or, if one broaches the simulation, one sees things as they are illuminated. Without quite seeing the light itself, one sees how it comes to illuminate things: they let one almost see light itself.

Among things, those that perhaps best let one almost see light itself are things that refuse the light, things that, being absolutely impenetrable to it, can only give it back in what seems the strictest of economies. They are things that gather light on their surface while prohibiting even the slightest transmission beneath that surface, concentrating the light precisely by requiring that it remain utterly superficial. They are things capable only of letting it shine on and from their surface, enhancing its intensity in the very refusal of it.

As with a stone protruding from the earth into brilliant sunlight.

Protruding from that matrix that is the very paradigm of closedness, of the inexorably self-secluded. Even as it protrudes into the open, the stone simulates this closure. Precisely in exposing its various surfaces to the light, it withdraws itself from them, draws itself—concentrates itself—into a sheer interior to which the surfaces give no access, an interior that they utterly obscure, in a sense that is no longer merely the symmetrical opposite of illumination.

The stone can become a measure for the light, can come to give a measure of the intensity of its shining. Looking at a surface of the stone, one also sees, precisely on that surface, the brilliance of the light that it gathers and concentrates, the brilliance with which the light shines from that surface. It seems hardly fortuitous that the very word by which one says the brilliance of light is etymologically linked, through the Latin (*berillus*, *beryllus*), to the name of a certain so-called precious stone (beryl).

In measuring—and in continuing to measure—the brilliance of shining, the stone also measures the progression of light, from twilight on through the successive times of day. It measures this progression not only by the brilliance of the shining concentrated on its surface but also by the ever varying distribution and configuration with which light is spread over the various surfaces. To say nothing of the shadow cast by the stone on the otherwise illuminated area around it. In measuring this progression, the stone at the same time measures that of the light's source, measures the progression of the sun across the sky. Especially (though not only) in casting its shadow—above all, if protruding into a widely open expanse—the stone is a natural clock, a clock already (as if) fabricated in the very thick of nature. Set by nature within nature, the natural clock produced by this lithography awaits the arrival of one capable of reading the measure it gives. Hence, the stone is a kind of book of nature, if in a different sense; it is a natural site of reading. Here one can read the time of day.

And yet, the preeminent natural clock is the sun itself. However the time of day may come to be measured, its first measure is the one inscribed across the sky, the course of the sun as it makes its way across that expanse, as its illumination grants the possibility of sight, satisfies the human need for sight and for the light that makes it possible. Time is the time of light, the time when it is light to some degree or other and in some manner or other—or even when it is no longer light and one can only await the sun's return, simulating in sleep the supervening darkness. Time is granted by the celestial source of light, by the movement of its uranic origin.

▼ ● ◆

But would such uranic time not be other than the time of philosophy? Would it not be, for philosophy, within all that philosophy has opened, an other time?

What would be required, then, in order to open philosophy to an other time? Assuming for the moment that one can appropriately say of time that it is or at least that there is (*il y a*) time, what would be required in order to open philosophy to the affirmation that there is a time other than the time of philosophy, a time that, being other, would be—alongside the time of philosophy—another time? What would be required, still further, to open it to the possibility of there being still another, still others, not just two but a number of others? What could warrant setting aside the assumption—seldom challenged in the history of philosophy—that time is singular? What could warrant setting aside even the assumption that, if there are multiple times, they are nonetheless in the final account all gathered into a single time, so that in the end the singularity of time would still be preserved? Can one be assured of the efficacy of such a gathering? Can one be assured that the time of a dream, the time of imagining, and the time of madness can all be reclaimed and reintegrated into a single all-encompassing, all-governing time? Can one be assured also that the times of elemental nature can be gathered and integrated into this single time? Can one be assured that the time of day and the time of year, that is, the times told by the most natural of clocks, the sun, can be brought to coincide, without remainder, with the times of the soul and of history? Or would there perhaps remain outside any such singular time as such, outside any time regarded as constituting time as such, an irrepressible trace of other times?

The question of the singularity of time is thus linked to the question of the *as such* of time, to the question whether there is an *as such* of time and hence a time as such. By putting in question the *as such* of time, one destabilizes in advance the question "What is time?" For in opening the question of the *as such* of time, one opens the possibility that time may be such as to have no single, coherent *what*, that there may be no such essence of time. Within such an opening, one cannot but prove already to have gone astray in posing the question of time in the form of the question "What is time?" One would not simply have posed a completely neutral question but rather—as perhaps always—would in the very formulation of the question already have responded to a certain preunderstanding, which could also involve misunderstanding, errancy.

And yet, the question cannot merely be put aside, if for no other reason than that it is precisely the question that Western philosophy has almost always put to time. If the question is limited, if the project of delimiting time as such, of determining its essence, is bound by certain limits, then those limits can be exposed only—or, at least, most effectively—by entering into the question and following it through in the most radical way, thus forcing to the limit the singularity and identity that philosophy has ascribed to time. Such a move to the limit would broach an exceeding of the time of philosophy—indeed in both senses.

▼ ● ◆

What, then, is time?

The question comes much too late. It is of course a citation from a text handed down across an enormous expanse of time, a text thus itself peculiarly entangled in that about which it poses this question. It is not only a text that was written a long time ago but also one that has been taken up time and time again, appropriated in and to times for which the confessional character of this text cannot but be alien and even disturbing.

Yet for Augustine, even in confession, the question is disturbing.

Augustine does not take the question for granted. Even if he never openly puts the question in question, he does attest to its force, to its recoil upon the questioner. His first response to it in the *Confessions* is to express how disturbing, how baffling a question it is: "What, then, is time? I know well enough what it is, provided that nobody asks me; but if I am asked what it is and try to explain, I am baffled."[1]

---

1. St. Augustine, *Confessions*, XI.14. I have used the Latin text of Book XI (with German translation) in Kurt Flasch, *Was ist Zeit?* (Frankfurt a.M.: Vittorio Klostermann, 1993). For some passages I have adapted the translation by R. S. Pine-Coffin (St. Augustine, *Confessions* [New York: Penguin Books, 1961]). Subsequent references to the *Confessions* are given by book and chapter numbers alone.

Thus the question, when it intervenes, disturbs one's assurance about time, the assurance with which one uses and understands the word *tempus*: "We certainly understand what is meant by the word both when we use it ourselves and when we hear it used by others" (XI.14). By disturbing this assurance, the posing of the question attests to the strangeness of the sense of time, that one has a sense of time, which, on the other hand, remains elusive and resists being drawn out and expressed as such.

But what, then, *is* time? What can it be said *to be*? Can it be said to be? It seems not, at least not without restrictions so severe as to reduce its sense of being almost to that of not being. For that part of time called past is no longer, and the part called future is not yet. Neither past nor future can be said to be. But the other part, the present, is a part of time rather than eternity only because it moves on to become the past. But, Augustine writes: "How can we say that even the present *is*, when the reason why it *is* is that it is *not to be*? In other words, we cannot rightly say that time *is*, except by reason of its impending state of *not being*" (XI.14).

One cannot even say that time *is* in part. For of its three parts, none simply *is*. The one part that cannot be declared nothing at all falls short of being nothing at all only by the very slightest of differences. Instead of not being, it is not to be. It is (not nothing) only by virtue of its impending not being. Its being borders on not being; its being is determined as such by reference to not being, to its impending not being.

It could be undermined even more disturbingly. As determined by reference to its impending not being, the present is constitutively linked to both of the other parts of time, those that simply are not: for to say that it is not to be—that its not being impends—is to say that in the future (which is not) it will be past (which is not). Or one could say, more precisely: at any moment whatsoever in the future it will have become past. One could also say, reciprocally, doubling the bond: in the past (which is not) it was future (which is not)—that is, at any moment whatsoever in the past it was still future. The present is what in the future will be past and in the past was future. This double bond to not being is constitutive for the present, constitutive of the present. Only by virtue of being doubly bound between the not being of the past and that of the future can the present be said—in some small measure—to be. And it is only in this same measure that time as such can be said to be.

It would not suffice, then, to say that time borders on not being, that time is almost nothing. For even the one moment of time that can be said, in some small measure, to be—namely, the present—*is* only by virtue of its constitutive bond to moments that *are not*. The present would be constituted as *being* (in some small measure) only by being set back upon the double void of past and future.

As if the present were nothing but the double bond to the past (which is nothing) and the future (which is nothing). As if the present were nothing but the double bond to nothing.

As if it were not also the moment of presence. Not only by being the moment in which things are present to one's vision but also by being itself determined through the measure that things can give.

As with a stone protruding from the earth into brilliant sunlight.

▼ ● ◆

In the *Confessions*, indeed in the very passage in which the present is linked constitutively to the double not being of past and future, there is an indication, slight but unmistakable, that the value of presence remains in force. Augustine writes: "As for the present, if it were always present and never moved on to become the past [*in praeteritum transirit*], it would not be time but eternity" (XI.14). For Augustine this difference is all-decisive. Only by differentiating time from eternity can he put aside once and for all the question of those fickle-minded interrogators whose thoughts go astray into questions such as that of what God was doing before he created the world. Only by way of this difference can he come to hear and understand—as he prays he might hear and understand—the meaning of the words: In the beginning you made heaven and earth (XI.3).

▼ ● ◆

The difference between time and eternity is a Platonic legacy, one that was established largely through the interpretation given in Middle Platonism to the Platonic phrase "moving image of eternity." This phrase is found in the discussion of time in the *Timaeus*, specifically in the expression: "The thought occurred to him [the god] of making a moving image of eternity [εἰκὼ δ' ἐπινοεῖ κινητόν τινα αἰῶνος ποιῆσαι]" (37d). The interpretation given in Middle Platonism identifies this moving image of eternity as time, and with Plotinus the conception of time as the moving image of eternity comes to be fixed as the Platonic definition of time. This determination is further enforced by restriction of the sense of the word αἰών, which in Classical Greek could also signify a lifetime, a generation, as well as a period of time of indefinite length. In the *Timaeus*, in particular, the word is determined by the phrase μένοντος . . . ἐν ἑνί (abiding . . . in unity), and so it signifies primarily remaining one and the same, remaining selfsame. There is no indication that in the Platonic text αἰών has the sense of a present that never passes, of eternal presence—the sense that will later be reinforced by the translation *aeternitas*, the sense that with Augustine is already thoroughly established.[2]

Here, then, it is a matter of a Platonic legacy that came to be utterly reconstituted in the early history of Platonism. Once the differentiation between time and eternity had been thus established, earlier echoes of the Platonic determination became inaudible, as Augustine attests when he writes: "I once heard a learned man say that time is nothing but the movement of the sun and the moon and the stars, but I did not agree" (XI.23).[3]

▼ ● ◆

Augustine never doubts the distinction between time and eternity. Indeed the very opening of Book XI declares the difference; it does so

2. This history has been thoroughly analyzed by Rémi Brague, *Du Temps chez Platon et Aristote* (Paris: Presses Universitaires de France, 1982), 11–27. See also my discussion of the passage on time (*Timaeus* 37d) in *Chorology*, 77–85.

3. Augustine goes on to counter that other movements could even more readily be identified with time; he offers the counterhypothesis that if all the lights of the sky ceased to move, the movement of the potter's wheel and of speech itself would still be in time. Scripture is also invoked: "I cannot therefore accept the suggestion that time is constituted by the movement of heavenly bodies, because although the sun once stood still in answer to a man's prayer [see *Jos.* 10:13], so that he could fight on until victory was his, the sun indeed stood still but time continued to pass." From the attestation of such an event, time's continual passage even as the sun stood still, Augustine moves directly to his concept of time as *distentio*: "I see time, therefore, as a distention of some sort" (XI.23).

through its way of declaring its own confessional intent. Since God is in eternity, either he is unaware of the things in time that are told to him or he sees in time the things that occur in it. In neither case will God learn of these things through the confession offered to him, for the difference between time and eternity will necessitate either that communication fails or that it proves superfluous. Confession is neither communication nor instruction. Rather, it is undertaken only to fire one's own heart and the hearts of readers, written only for love of God's love (XI.1).

Declared from the outset, the difference between time and eternity is then to be understood. This understanding comes well in advance of the passage that links the present to the not being of past and future. Or rather, Augustine first expresses what fundamentally determines the difference and then, in the later passage and on the basis thus provided, explicates the constitution of time.

The difference is a difference of presence, a differentiation with regard to presence. Augustine writes: "In eternity nothing moves into the past, but all is present [*sed totum esse praesens*]. Time, on the other hand, is never all present at once" (XI.11). Even eternity is determined by the present, by the value of presence. Eternity is an absolutely unlimited present, a present that does not move into the past; it is a present that will not in the future have become past and that has not in the past been still future. Eternity is present, and what differentiates the present from eternity is only that the present *of time* is constitutively bound to the not being—that is, the non-presence—of the past and the future. Thus, to say that "the present is time only by reason of the fact that it moves on to become the past" (XI.14)—that is, only by virtue of its impending not being—is *not* to say that the present (and, hence, time as such) is constituted solely by the bond to the not being of past and future. Rather, it is to say that the present is a present *of time*—rather than the present of eternity—by virtue of its bond to the not being (that is, the non-presence) of the past and the future. Even if the present of time is submitted constitutively to its impending not being (present), it is still—decisively, constitutively—*present*.

The constitutive value of presence not only for eternity but also for the temporal present and even for the future and the past is unmistakably attested by the way in which all these modes are brought back to *praesens* and accorded their being, at least to some degree, on this basis. And what of *praesens* itself? To what is it brought back? What is its locus? Where is it that everything present becomes present?

It is from this question—the question of the *where* (*ubi*), itself legitimated as a question by the value of presence (whatever is present is present somewhere)—that Augustine proceeds: "If the future and the past are, I want to know where they are" (XI.18). Deferring the question of the *where*, Augustine declares that future and past, if they *are* in any measure, are present. Wherever they may be, "they are not there as future or past but as present," for the future is not yet and the past is no longer. His conclusion: "Wherever they are and whatever they are, it is only by being present that they are" (XI.18). Only insofar as the *future is present* can it be whatsoever (whatever it be) and be somewhere; and likewise for the past. Yet how can the future and the past be present without the very differentiation of time into three parts being effaced? And in this case would not the very distinction between time and eternity be abolished? For what distinguishes time from eternity is precisely that its present is constitutively bound to the not being of the future and the past. But if this difference is abolished, then the entire situation of confession will collapse into one of communication, at best, or else into one of arrogant self-assertion. Here it is evident how intrinsically the form and content of confession are bound together.

How can the future and the past be present while remaining, respectively, future and past? This is possible only by virtue of what could be called the intentional or apertural structure of the present (gathered in the word *praesens*, in what for us is its double meaning): the present is a moment of presence, a moment in which vision is opened upon things present. But how can things not present—namely, the future and the past—nonetheless be somehow present? Only if, while not being present as such, they are held in a place that accords them a certain presence, a place that shelters them from not being, a place that is such that to be there in that place, in that receptacle, is to be present. Then it can be said that, though the future and the past are not, there are nonetheless three times: a present of the past (*praesens de praeteritis*), a present of the present (*praesens de praesentibus*), and a present of the future (*praesens de futuris*). Or, since no differentiation is inscribed between, for instance, the past and what is past (that is, those things or events that belong to the past), nor of course between present and presence, the three times can also be delimited as: a presence of what is past, a presence of what is present, and a presence of what is future.

Augustine is thus brought back to the question of the *where* of time, that is, of the place where each of the parts of time would be sheltered from not being and so would be present. Augustine takes this place to be the soul, and this means also that he takes the soul to be the only such place. As a way of securing the differentiation of times (and hence of time from eternity), Augustine takes the soul to be the place of time, its *where*. This setting of time in its *where* cannot have the sense of a mere subordination of time to place, but rather its sense must be such as to erode this very distinction in the direction of a reception and a receptacle that, with a precedence neither spatial nor temporal, would precede all determination of places and of times—even though this sense of precedence never becomes manifest or thematized in Augustine's confessional text.

Whatever its precedence, Augustine is assured that the place of time is the soul: "Some such different times do exist in the soul [*sunt . . . in anima*], but nowhere else that I can see. The present [presence—*praesens*] of what is past is memory [*memoria*]; the present of what is present is beholding [*contuitus*]; the present of what is future is expectation [*expectatio*]" (XI.20).

Different times are (present) only in the soul, Augustine thus insists, "but nowhere else that I can see."

As if future and past were not etched into the things that nature sets before our vision.

As in the cherry blossoms that have not yet quite come forth. As in the maple leaves that have only begun to turn yellowish orange. As these things are set before our vision.

Or as a stone protruding from the earth is marked with a past that has never been present in memory, a past older than any memory.

▼ ● ◆

How is it that, for Augustine, it is in the soul—"but nowhere else that I can see"—that time has its place? How does the soul provide time with its *where*, with a place where it is sheltered from not being? By way of what operations does the soul grant to time a place to be?

The future has its place, its presence, in expectation, through this operation and the power that makes it possible. Likewise with the past: it has its place in memory, is granted its presence through this operation and its enabling power. What, then, about the present? Must it, too, be sheltered from not being? Must it, too, be granted its presence by an operation of the soul? Or is it not, precisely as present, itself inalienably present? Does it not suffice that the present is the very opening to presence? Is there need to submit even the present to an operation of the soul in order to assure it its presence? Is there need to double the present into a presence of the present? Is there need to double its opening upon presence, to double it by reference back to an operation of the soul, an operation *in* the soul, that would shelter the present from not being?

Augustine is convinced that there is such a need. Why? Because the present has no space, no extent—a thesis that he is confident no one would deny: "Again, no one would deny that the present has no extent [*spatium*], since it *is* only at the point of its passage [*in puncto praeterit*]" (XI.28). It would be difficult to exaggerate the force of this thesis, the force of its consequences of course but also the force with which it is made to exclude a certain *spatium* that the present could otherwise be taken to have: the space of its opening upon presence, the extent of its extendedness to the things that nature sets before our vision. One would presume even that it is by virtue of this *spatium* that the present is so akin to eternity that the latter is determined by the value of presence, determined as unlimited presence ("In eternity . . . all is present"), determined as a present to which absolutely unlimited *spatium* belongs.

But if, as Augustine is convinced, there is no *spatium* of the present, then an operation of the soul must come to shelter it from the not being of being only at the point of its passage. An operation of the soul must come to supply the present with a *spatium* of presence in order that it can *be*, in order that there be presence of the present. Augustine calls that operation *attentio*, and not, as in the previous passage (XI.20), *contuitus*: "Yet, [the soul's] attentiveness persists [*perdurat attentio*], and through it that which is to be passes toward the state in which it is to be no more" (XI.28). It is as if Augustine were concerned that merely beholding (*contuitus*) might not suffice to give a *spatium* and so a presence to its present. Or rather, at least, such beholding would need to be redoubled so that one not only beheld something but held that very beholding in mind, held it in a perduring attentiveness capable of granting it a *spatium*. In the end, the present would have no extent other than that of the soul's operation of perdurant attentiveness.

Augustine broaches this end when, translating Plotinus' διάστασις[4] into *distentio*, he ventures to identify the extending, the stretching out, denoted by this word, to identify it as constituting the very *what* of time. Augustine writes: "It seems to me, then, that time is merely a distention, though of what it is a distention I do not know" (XI.26). And yet, if *distentio* designates the movement through which intervals of presence are installed within the otherwise incessant flight of what is to be into what has been, if *distentio* names not just this flight but its presence, that is, the presence and extent granted it by memory, attentiveness, and expectation, then this *distentio* will be inseparable from these operations of the soul. It will perhaps be even *of the soul*: "I begin to wonder whether it is a distention of the soul itself" (XI.26).

Transformed into the distention of the soul, withdrawn into the soul as the only place thought capable of sheltering it from not being, time will be deprived of its direct engagement with things. Thus withdrawn from things, time will no longer be taken to impart itself to their comings and goings; or, at best, it will seem to do so only secondarily, only subsequent to its proper constitution, in an order of precedence that would no longer be that even of time itself. For Augustine time can be sheltered from not being only through being doubled in the soul, only through being doubled by the three dyadic forms: presence of the past, presence of the present, and presence of the future. Once the time in which things come to pass has been doubled by this other time within the soul, the reversal is inevitable: as the time sheltered from not being, as the time that can be said to be, this other time within the soul will be taken, not as the mere double or doubling of another time, but as the original, as time itself, as originary time.

Even short of this reversal, the withdrawal from things will make time seem quite immune to their touch, effectively protected from contamination by them.

---

4. "The spreading out [διάστασις] of life involves time" (Plotinus, *Ennead* III.7.11).

As if time, in being distended to the point of being distention as such, were not also gathered in the present opening to things. As if time were not extended also to things, stretching around them, as it were, embracing them. As if time, the very movement of being-outside-itself, were not properly outside itself (outside *its* outside), indeed so thoroughly as to efface the difference separating it from the outside. As if time were not there amidst things.

As if time's being amidst things were not attested by the things themselves, by their giving a measure by which time is determined. As the sun provides the measure for the time of day.

▼ ● ◆

No turn was more decisive than that by which the interrogation of time was made to issue the imperative that time be submitted to the question of being and that consequently it be exposed to the possibility of not being, to the possibility of its being not only drawn into not being but even withdrawn to such an extent as to lose all common measure with the things that come into being and pass away into not being. Thus the question to be addressed to time, to each of its parts, became that of whether and how each part of time *is* and of how, if no part of time truly *is*, time as such can *be*. Not that this became the sole question: the question of whether and how time and its parts *are* cannot be pursued without other questions imposing themselves, above all, the question of *what* time is. Yet the question of *what* time *is* is not just another question: for every classical determination of the *what* (*essentia*, εἶδος) is inseparable from the determination of being, to such a degree that, at least within the horizon of the classical determinations, one cannot ask the question of *what* time *is* without thereby submitting time to the question of being. Thus, the primary question to be posed to time was, from the time of the Greeks, the question of being. From the Greeks on, it will have been a question only of being and time.

And yet—

A certain intimation of time was already in play, and through this intimation time came to determine the very sense of being itself. In a decisive respect Heidegger's thought can be said even to proceed precisely from this insight: that the meaning of being was determined by the Greeks as presence, as *Anwesenheit*.[5] Thus was it determined for what now, precisely with a view back to this determination, one tends to call the history of metaphysics. Yet for all its decisiveness, the determination was not itself thematized as such. Brought to bear on the determination of being as such, the temporal determination goes—proves to have gone—unthematized in its character as temporal.

Thus the turn by which time is submitted to the question of being is more entangling than it would have seemed. In posing as primary the question of the being of time, one turns indeed in a circle; one is set circling around toward the time of being. Having been brought to bear on the determination of the meaning of being, time is then submitted to that very meaning; from the moment time is interrogated primarily as regards its being, it is submitted to that very meaning that it will have determined.

Only when this circle becomes manifest as such, only when it becomes thematic that time is the meaning of being—only then does the withdrawal of time into the soul become radically questionable. Only then will one also be led to ask again about the engagement of time with things, with their coming and going.

In another time. In a time when time will have been released to things.

▼ ● ◆

It is Heidegger who has radicalized to the limit the sheltering of time within the soul, its being of the soul. Thereby he has also forced to the limit the singularity and identity that philosophy has ascribed, if only tacitly, to time. Most transparent in this regard is Heidegger's 1924 lecture *The Concept of Time*: referring explicitly to the *Confessions* and to the question that Augustine pursued concerning the identity of time with the soul, Heidegger renews the interrogation and comes finally to a conclusion that radicalizes to the limit the place-

5. See Heidegger's Preface to William J. Richardson, *Heidegger: Through Phenomenology to Thought* (The Hague: Martinus Nijhoff, 1963), xiii.

ment of time in the soul.[6] Setting aside the classical determination of that being that we ourselves are, redetermining it as Dasein, Heidegger declares that time is Dasein, that Dasein is temporality. Correspondingly, Heidegger traces the displacement undergone by the question "What is time?"—its transformation into the question "Who is time?" and finally into the question "Am I my time?"[7] *Being and Time* carries through in a thorough and rigorous way the identity declared in the lecture: in *Being and Time* all the existential structures and even the opening of the world are brought back to their ground in temporality, which is the meaning of the being of Dasein. The question is whether, in forcing the singularity and identity of time to the limit, Heidegger also initiates their disruption. And whether, following Heidegger to this limit, one could at least warrant opening the question of another time.

In any case Heidegger's project could not but have a significant bearing on the Augustinian sheltering of time from not being and on the consequent installing of time in the soul, its determination as of the soul. For both the need to shelter from not being and the appeal to the doubling of time as the means of sheltering it proceed on the basis of an understanding of *being as presence*. Since Heidegger's project in its most global parameters is to put in question the meaning of being, indeed, above all, to put in question the understanding of being as presence that has governed Western philosophy since the Greeks, his project cannot but recoil upon and begin to erode that very Augustinian analysis that, on the other hand, he carries through to its completion. The Platonic legacy that was already thoroughly transformed by the time of Augustine is, at once, radicalized and unsettled in *Being and Time*.

---

6. In the notes (unpublished) of a lecture given on 26 October 1930 at the Beuron monastery entitled "Des hl. Augustinus Betrachtung über die Zeit. Confessiones lib. XI," Heidegger draws the very closest connection between Augustine's *distentio* and his own determination of Dasein's temporality as *Sicherstrecken*. One passage reads: "Der Geist selbst erstreckt sich; ich selbst bin, indem ich mich erstrecke. Diese distentio bildet sich, sie bildet die tensio. Dieses ihr Bilden ist ihr Wesen. Der distentionale Charakter der Zeit." Another passage: "tempus ist distentio—memoria, expectatio, contuitus. (positiv) das dreifach gestreute Sicherstrecken: Behalten, Erwarten, Gegenwärtigen; das bildet—als blickbares Bild. Vergangenheit, Zukunft, Gegenwart."

7. Martin Heidegger, *Der Begriff der Zeit* (Tübingen: Max Niemeyer, 1989), 26–28.

▼ ● ◆

Being and Time was not simply to have ended with the temporality of Dasein. On the contrary, the analytic was to have advanced beyond Dasein and temporality to time and being. Even though this final analytic would have been developed from the temporal interpretation of Dasein, it would nonetheless have constituted an advance by bringing to light time "as the horizon for all understanding of being" (SZ, 17).[8] The final move would, then, have been from temporality as the meaning of the being of Dasein to time as the horizon for all understanding of being. Set within this horizon, understood from it, being would be exhibited in its temporal character. In order to indicate that such a temporal character could not consist merely in being in time as beings can be said to be in time, Heidegger designates it by the Latin cognate *temporal*, in distinction from *zeitlich*. Indeed, he marks the advance as such by differentiating between *die Zeitlichkeit des Daseins* and *die Temporalität des Seins*. He writes: "The determination of the meaning of being and of its characters and modes on the basis of time we call its *temporal* determination [*seine* temporale *Bestimmtheit*]. Thus the fundamental ontological task of interpreting being as such includes working out the *temporality of being* [Temporalität des Seins]. In the exposition of the problematic of temporality [*Temporalität*] the question of the meaning of being will first be concretely answered" (SZ, 19).

This advance from *Zeitlichkeit* to *Temporalität* was of course never carried out. In its published form *Being and Time* breaks off at the end of the analysis of Dasein and *Zeitlichkeit*, breaks off with a series of questions about this very advance that has not been carried out: "Is there a way leading from originary *time* to the meaning of *being*? Does *time* itself reveal itself as the horizon of *being*?" (SZ, 437).

From these indications and from the elaborations found in Heidegger's lectures from the late 1920s, it is difficult to determine the precise character of the advance from *Zeitlichkeit* to *Temporalität*. Yet, whatever its specific character, it would be an advance to a form

8. All references to *Being and Time* (indicated by SZ followed by page number) are to the ninth German edition: *Sein und Zeit*, 9th, unaltered edition (Tübingen: Max Niemeyer, 1960).

of time that would be more originary than the originary time of Dasein. It would be an advance beyond the time that the existential analysis establishes in its identity with Dasein, an advance beyond the time that would be sheltered in what was once called the soul, an advance toward another time. It is the question of such an advance that needs to be pursued in order to drive Heidegger's analysis to the limit where perhaps a first glimpse of another time may be offered; and though the advance will turn out to proceed along a way different from that to which Heidegger alludes in his all too brief discourses on *Temporalität*, it will be broached largely on the basis of certain particular indications found in Heidegger's text.

If there is another time that, like *Temporalität*, is beyond—or rather, before—Dasein's temporality, then this other time will also be anterior to Dasein's historicity, which is founded on Dasein's temporality. This other time, this time before time, could, then, appropriately be called prehistorical time. But in this designation it remains to be determined what the *pre-* signifies, that is, what the sense of anteriority must be.

▼ ● ◆

In a sense Dasein's temporality is prehistorical, is anterior to history. In this regard anteriority refers to the order of founding: temporality is what makes possible Dasein's occurrence (*Geschehen*), and the latter, in turn, is what founds history in all its various senses. Yet, precisely by being in this sense prehistorical, temporality as such is thoroughly historical. Dasein's time is historical time.

Heidegger's analysis in this regard focuses on Dasein's occurrence (*Geschehen*). To Dasein there belongs a certain extending (*Erstreckung*): Dasein extends itself or is itself extended from birth to death, or, perhaps better, there is an extending of Dasein from birth to death; this extending is what constitutes the connectedness of life.[9] This specific movement of extending is what Heidegger calls the occurrence (*Geschehen*) of Dasein. The structure of Dasein's occurrence (*Geschehen*) is called historicity (*Geschichtlichkeit*). In the most rigorous terms, it is

9. See, above, n. 6.

historicity that is founded on, made possible by, temporality. This relation is perhaps most evident in Heidegger's description of the originary mode of Dasein's occurrence, which he calls fate (*Schicksal*): Dasein's occurrence in this mode is geared to its being freed, through authentic being-toward-death, so that it chooses to choose among the possibilities that, as thrown, it finds handed down to it, so that, in Heidegger's words, "Dasein, free for death, hands itself down to itself in a possibility that it has inherited and yet has chosen" (*SZ*, 384). In being-toward-death there lies the future, in being thrown amidst handed-down possibilities there lies having-been (*Gewesenheit*), and in taking over and choosing there lies the present. Heidegger's conclusion: fate—and, more generally, Dasein's occurrence as such—"requires, as the ontological condition of its possibility, the constitution of being of care [*die Seinsverfassung der Sorge*], that is, temporality" (*SZ*, 385). In short, temporality is the condition of the possibility of Dasein's occurrence, that is, of historicity. And, as Heidegger also shows, everything to which the word *history*—the two words *Geschichte* and *Historie*—is extended comes back finally to Dasein's historicity.

On the one hand, then, Heidegger sets temporality before history by exposing it as the condition of the possibility of history. But, on the other hand, Heidegger also closes the gap that might otherwise be taken to separate condition from conditioned. The analysis of historicity, he says "merely reveals what already lies enveloped in the temporalizing of temporality" (*SZ*, 376). Thus, historicity is not anything other than temporality. As Heidegger says, still more directly: "Historicity as the constitution of the being of existence is 'fundamentally' temporality [*Geschichtlichkeit als Seinsverfassung der Existenz ist 'im Grunde' Zeitlichkeit*]" (*SZ*, 404). Therefore, while temporality is the condition of the possibility of historicity (and hence of history), it is nothing other than historicity, nothing set apart from and in this sense anterior to historicity. Dasein's time is as such historical time. And, since Dasein's time is originary time, there would be, in the final analysis, no prehistorical time.

And yet, there is something that would seem to limit the coincidence of temporality and historicity, something that, while also stemming from temporality, must be differentiated from historicity. Heidegger mentions the need and use of calendars and clocks, that is, a certain reckoning with time that is turned toward things and only remotely, if at all, linked to Dasein's historicity. Heidegger mentions too that whatever occurs along with it Dasein experiences as "in time." Heidegger singles out those things belonging to nature: the processes of nature, whether living or lifeless, are encountered as "in time." This time within which natural things occur is, to some extent at least, other than the time of history, even if this other time also has its origin finally in temporality. The analysis of this other time is thus coordinate with and independent of the analysis of historicity, so that, as Heidegger remarks, the analysis of how this time of within-timeness (*Innerzeitigkeit*) originates from temporality could just as easily be placed before, instead of after, the discussion of the connection between historicity and temporality. Heidegger declares even that, insofar as the time of within-timeness also stems from temporality, historicity and within-timeness are equally originary (*gleichursprünglich*) (*SZ*, 376f.). This other time in which things occur and with which Dasein reckons is another stem of temporality, irreducible to historicity even though linked to it through the common root, temporality. The question is one of gauging the withdrawal of this other time from the time of history and of determining its capacity to resist assimilation to Dasein's historicity. Can this crack in the hegemony of history be opened to such an extent as to expose a time that is prehistorical in the most radical sense?

▼ ● ◆

The final chapter of *Being and Time* opens with another reference to Dasein's reckoning with time, this reckoning now being characterized as an elemental comportment, which, Heidegger insists, must be clarified before it can be determined what is meant in saying that beings are "in time." It is not just that a dimension of the phenomenon of temporality remains unconsidered; rather, the analysis of temporality remains, says Heidegger, incomplete specifically because it has not yet shown how "something like world-time [*Weltzeit*] in the rigorous sense of the existential-temporal concept of world belongs to temporality itself" (*SZ*, 405). Heidegger already alludes to what will become evident in the course of the analysis to come: world-time is the time *in which* beings occur; it is the time by virtue of which they have their within-timeness (*Innerzeitigkeit*). The question to be addressed is, then, that of the relation between Dasein's most elemental reckoning with time and the constitution of world-time.

Heidegger does not, however, address this question directly. Instead of an analysis of world-time as such, what Heidegger proceeds to develop is an analysis of what he calls *die besorgte Zeit*. This time, another time to be distinguished both from that of historicity and from temporality, is a time of concern in two senses. It is, first of all, the time that belongs to the sphere of circumspective concern, the time constituted, as it were, within this sphere. But, secondly, it is also the time with which Dasein can be concerned, the time to which Dasein's concern can be directed, as, for instance, in reckoning with time.

Heidegger's analysis undertakes to show how the time of concern arises from—is constituted on the basis of—temporality, which by this demonstration, says Heidegger, would thus also be shown to be *originary time*, granted, as Heidegger will easily show, that the ordinary concept of time as a sequence of nows arises, in turn, from the time of concern. Granted, too, that no other time becomes manifest, no other time that would fall outside the order of founding: now-time founded on the time of concern, and the time of concern founded on temporality, thus shown to be originary time. Granted, then, that world-time also can be accommodated to this order of founding.

How does the time of concern arise from temporality? Heidegger's answer is explicit: by self-interpretation. In other words, the time of concern is self-interpreted temporality; it is temporality set interpretively before itself, an interpretive doubling of temporality.

The contours of Heidegger's analysis in this regard can be readily sketched. In circumspective concern Dasein is engaged with the things at hand (*das Zuhandene*) within the world. Dasein understands these things, that is, projects them upon their world-horizon; Dasein interprets them, exhibits them *as* something in relation to the meanings granted them by the horizon; Dasein discourses about them, articulating the context of meaning, and expresses this discourse in language, addressing itself to these things. Yet these things at hand are not objects over against Dasein such that in speaking of them Dasein could leave entirely out of its account its own comportment to them. On the contrary, in interpreting and speaking of the things at hand, Dasein cannot but also interpret and express its own being-alongside them. In Dasein's comportment to them, in circumspective concern, there is always self-interpretation and self-expression; that is, in such comportment Dasein is always disclosed to itself with some degree of transparency, disclosed to itself in a self-interpreted form, that is, as a form of temporality. The time of concern is precisely the form in which temporality is set before itself through the self-interpretation and self-expression that occur in circumspective concern. The time of concern is the form that self-interpreted temporality assumes in the sphere of circumspective concern.

What is this form of time? How does the temporality of circumspective concern interpret itself, that is, within what horizon, within what context of meanings? Heidegger's answer is not entirely univocal: in circumspective concern Dasein interprets its temporality, interprets itself as temporality, by reference to the world *or*, as Heidegger's actual descriptions bear out, by reference to the things and events at hand within the world. For example: *now that* I reach for the right tool so that what I am making will be finished *when later* someone comes for it, I find the tool just where it was *when formerly* I used it. In this interpretation there is operative what Heidegger calls an assigning or giving of time (*Zeitangabe*): Dasein assigns its temporality to its concrete, factical being-alongside things at hand, transposes temporality into a time of its concern with things at hand. Furthermore, by setting temporality—that is, itself as temporality—into the field of things at hand, Dasein gives time to itself, gives itself a time with which it can be concerned, with which it can reckon. There is, then, a *double giving of time*: Dasein gives, assigns, time to the things and events at hand within the world so as thereby to give to itself the time of concern. Thus, the reckoning that would be a genuinely elemental comportment would have the character of a double giving of time.

Yet the time of concern, constituted in and through this double giving, is not yet—not quite—world-time. Heidegger says that in order for world-time to arise from the time of concern the latter must have been made public (*SZ*, 414). This being made public cannot consist simply in others' coming to share the time of concern; for other Daseins will always already have been there all along (Dasein as *Mitsein*), and, accordingly, the time of concern would never have been a solitary time that an isolated Dasein would then come to share with others. But what is it, then, that makes time public? What is it that brings about the advance from the time of concern to world-time?

Although the time of concern can arise through self-interpretation simply in reference to the things and events at hand within the environing world (*Umwelt*), Heidegger indicates that there is a further horizon that comes into play, a horizon that bears on time's becoming public, its becoming world-time. This other horizon is that of the kind of concern with time that we are familiar with as astronomical and calendrical time-reckoning (*SZ*, 411). Orientation to this other horizon Heidegger links to Dasein's thrownness, to such an extent that he declares thrownness to be the reason why there is time publicly.

Heidegger's analysis proceeds from the need for sight. Circumspective concern needs the possibility of sight; its double giving of time, one may add, likewise is submitted to this need, so that in the giving of time this need for sight must be taken into account. Above all, this means that in its thrownness Dasein is submitted to the alternation of day and night, the brightness of day giving this possibility of sight, night taking it away. Hence, the double giving of time, which operates within circumspective concern and constitutes the time of concern, cannot take place without reference beyond the environing world of that concern; it cannot take place without also referring—or rather, submitting—to the gift of light bestowed by the heaven, preeminently by the sun. Designating the assigning of time as a matter of dating, Heidegger declares: "The sun dates the time that is interpreted in concern." He continues: "From this dating arises the 'most natural' measure of time, the day." In turn, he says, the dividing up of the day is "carried out with regard to that by which time is dated: the journeying sun" (*SZ*, 412f.). It is this dating—carried out from the heavenly bodies and their distinctive places in the sky—that makes time public, that makes it assignable in a way that we can share, as Heidegger says, "'under the same sky'" (*SZ*, 413). Thus, only in coming to be dated from the sky does the time of concern become world-time. Whereas Dasein gives time to environmental things and events, the sky gives time to Dasein and to its entire sphere of circumspective concern. Whereas, giving time to things at hand in circumspective concern, Dasein gives itself this time, sets itself before itself as this form of time, this double giving of time is submitted to the sky, is bound by that other time that the sky and, preeminently, its sun give to Dasein and its restricted, not-yet-public, indeed narrow sphere of circumspective concern.

In Heidegger's discussion of world-time, one finds the following, very remarkable declaration: "'Time' first shows itself in the sky, that is, precisely there where one comes across it in directing oneself naturally *according to it*, so that time even becomes identified with the sky" (*SZ*, 419). First showing itself in the sky, time—this other time, this uranic time—is anterior to the time that Dasein gives itself in circumspective concern, anterior to such a degree that it is from the sky that time is first given to this narrow sphere. Little wonder that this other time from above has even, as Heidegger says, been identified with the sky. For instance—the most compelling instance, though it is unlikely that Heidegger had it in mind—in Plato's *Timaeus*. It is back to this forgotten Platonic legacy that Heidegger's analysis—almost certainly without his having realized it—leads.

There is little reason to suppose that this other time, uranic time, could be assimilated to Dasein's historicity. One might rather suppose that its circling gives the time within which the time of history would arise, that it gives the time within which Dasein hands itself down to itself, just as it gives the time for Dasein's self-interpretation in circumspective concern.

The more difficult question is whether this uranic time can be appropriated to temporality, to its order of founding, so that temporality could still be declared originary time and the identity and singularity of time still preserved. Or whether uranic time is another time, whether it is a time that escapes the founding order, whether it is a time other than the temporality of Dasein, a time even that commands that temporality, a time other than human time, a time to which human time cannot but submit. An inexorable time.

Above all, it will be a question of whether the region that gives this other time can be assimilated to the existential structures, all of which lead back, in the founding order, to temporality. Yet one cannot but wonder whether it could ever suffice phenomenologically to regard the sun as no more than something at hand in a world delimited by human goals and possibilities or as something rendered objectively present (*vorhanden*) only by being deprived of the referential significations it would in the first instance have had in such a world. Is the inexorability of the sun as it traverses the sky not more insistent than any such things could ever be? To say nothing of the sky, which is not a thing at all, which shows itself in a showing in which the profile-structure belonging to all self-showings of things is completely effaced. Could the sheer radiance of the sky, its pure shining, the radiant shining that *is* the sky, ever be mistaken for something at hand in the narrow human world? Then, neither could the time it gives be assimilated to Dasein's temporality. And then, one would need to say that the time given by the sky, this uranic time, is, in a way both remote and wondrous, an other time.

▼ ● ◆

One can recall a time before time was withheld from things and deprived of the measure they can give it. One can recall a time before time was utterly withdrawn into the soul, a time when time was said to be inseparable from the heavens, a time when it was thought to be so manifestly there amidst things—especially those manifest in the sky (οὐρανός)—that one would have to say that time and these things were produced at the same time (the word ἅμα expressing this simultaneity precedent to temporal simultaneity). Not that the *Timaeus* denied that, in a sense, the soul is the site of time. Yet the soul—if this word, with all it has borne since, can still translate ψυχή—to which time belongs is not that of an individual human being; neither is it that in which the powers of a transcendental subject would inhere. Rather, it is to the soul *of the cosmos* that time belongs. Its site is preeminently the sky: Timaeus declares that the sun, the moon, and the planets "came into being for the determining and guarding of the numbers of time [εἰς διορισμὸν καὶ φυλακὴν ἀριθμῶν χρόνου γέγονε]" (*Tim.* 38c). These heavenly bodies, these uranic things, he calls the instruments or organs of time (ὄργανα χρόνου) (*Tim.* 42d).

Of uranic time.

Yet in the turn back to the forgotten Platonic legacy, to the legacy that, from Middle Platonism on, was withheld, was not handed down, even *uranic time* comes to border on tautology. For the moving image of the ever selfsame (of the αἰών), identified as time, is—to say the least—nothing other than the starry heaven.[10] Χρόνος is nothing other than οὐρανός.

▼ ● ◆

And yet—

With a stone protruding from the earth into brilliant sunlight it is not only a matter of uranic time, of a measure of such time, of giving a measure of such time.

As a quiet receptiveness comes over one's vision, descending upon it as the gift of opening, one will sense that the time *of* the stone

10. See *Chorology*, 77–85.

is other than the time it measures. One will sense that the time borne by the stone is not a time measured by the movement of the heavenly bodies but rather a time to which movement is absolutely alien, a time of utter repose, a time that is utter repose. A time withdrawn even more decisively from that of human events, a time that is neither of the sky nor of history.

A lithic time perhaps.

A time of the earth.

CHAPTER 7

WHAT'S THE MATTER WITH "NATURE"?

WHAT'S THE MATTER with "nature"?

The question is a citation, not my question—not at least in quite these words—but Charles Scott's question. This question serves to entitle the second chapter of Scott's book *The Lives of Things*.[1] Beyond this opening, entitling question and beyond the direct appeal to elemental nature, exemplified by a passage cited from Henry Beston's *The Outermost House*, the tone of the chapter is sounded and its primary orientation is defined, almost at the beginning, by a very remarkable phrase. Scott writes of "the differential distance of the unappropriable quality of events in their volatile presence with us" (23). With utter conciseness this phrase marks the two opposed moments that determine—that Scott would have us recognize as determining—all human comportment to the lives of things: on the one hand, their presence to us as they offer up sense in every sense; on the other hand, their unappropriable quality, which is thereby not a quality but rather a volatizing and distancing that renders their presence also unutterably different from the sense they offer us.

The second of these moments, that of difference, Scott regards as playing a significant role in the provocation of astonishment or wonder, by which I take him to be translating what in the *Theaetetus* Socrates calls θαυμάζειν, even if in a translation that is anything but

1. Charles E. Scott, *The Lives of Things* (Bloomington: Indiana University Press, 2002). References are given by page number within the text.

a simple, continuous transition from a sense in one language to the same sense expressed in another language. Socrates also calls this the ἀρχή of philosophy, a word that for the moment I will leave untranslated, since much of what I want to say by way of response to Scott's astonishing and wonderful book has to do precisely with ἀρχή. In any case, when Scott writes of astonishment or wonder, there is always reference to what he calls "the unspeakable wonder of lives." What, above all, provokes wonder is that lives, even when measured, are, in Scott's words, "forever breaking the measurements and shining in their passing intensities" (5). Here the word "lives" is almost entirely unrestricted; it is a matter of the lives of things. Indeed one would be tempted to say: the lives of things as such—were it not that Scott's work puts thoroughly in question the *as such* itself, the *as such* as such.

One could even say that, according to Scott, the hegemony of the *as such* that "nature" enforces is precisely what is the matter with "nature," what is wrong with it. The quotation marks in which, in the formulation of the question, Scott encloses nature function in at least two different ways. They serve, in the first place, to mark the questionableness of what is called and conceived as nature; they suggest that nature in this sense, with its claim to be the sense of nature as such, falls short of what one would like to call nature itself, were the significations both of nature and of its *itself* not already appropriated to and controlled by the very sense of nature in question. What is questionable about nature in this sense is its relation—a relation posited as nonrelation—to the unappropriable quality, the volatizing and distancing difference, that belongs to the lives of things. The quotation marks enclosing nature serve, secondly, to indicate that in the question "What's the matter with 'nature'?" it is primarily the word "nature" that is asked about, not that which the word presumes to name, though it would seem that nothing short of a recoil from what it presumes to name could suffice to put it in question and to initiate a marking of its limits. In asking about the word, one also asks about the signification, the concept of nature, that it puts into play.

What is wrong with "nature"—with the word and with its signification—is that it draws away, as Scott says, "from the concrete specificity of things and their happenings" (23). Drawing away—and drawing us away—from the lives of things, "nature" often draws us to the merely conceptual, to the abstract; in Scott's words, it "often draw[s] us to an abstracting process rather than to the lives of things," (23) to their concrete specificity or, more precisely, to the "singularities of things" in their "unspeakable differences" (30–31) from the sense they present to us. On the other hand, Scott grants that "nature" does not always draw in this way, that the word can be and is sometimes used with the opposite intention. In such cases the signification of "nature" would somehow point beyond what can be signified, beyond what can be represented in a concept of nature, beyond to the differentiated, unspeakable singularities.

There is perhaps no saying in advance or in general how such writing would be effected, but I think immediately of Beston and others like him. Whatever may remain unsaid and in remaining unsaid may threaten to divert the writing away from the lives of things, such writing—in its very singularity—succeeds in translating "nature" beyond its concept. As in the passage from Beston that Scott cites in part in and as the beginning of his own discourse on "What's the matter with 'nature'?": "[By the sea] the great rhythms of nature, today so dully disregarded, wounded even, have here their spacious and primeval liberty; cloud and shadow of cloud, wind and tide, tremor of night and day. Journeying birds alight here and fly away again all unseen, schools of great fish move beneath the waves, the surf flings its spray against the sun."[2] Also, as in another passage in which Beston writes of how today we lack—are oblivious to—elemental things, of our need "for fire before the hands, for water welling from the earth, for air, for the dear earth itself underfoot." Beston attests that in his "world of beach and dune these elemental presences lived and had their being, and under their arch there moved an incomparable pageant of nature and the year."[3]

Such writing can be almost uncanny in its capacity to draw us back to the strangeness, the unappropriable quality, of familiar things, especially when it is a matter of the prodigiousness of what I too—in a very different discourse—would call the *elemental*. Yet writing such as Beston's is other than philosophical and stands under no compulsion to venture to say that which holds—or rather, withholds—things in their singularity. Philosophical writing, on the other hand, addresses

---

2. Henry Beston, *The Outermost House* (1928; reprint, New York: Henry Holt, 1977), 2.

3. Ibid., 10.

this retreat of sense and thereby is augmented by a certain critical dimension that minimizes its exposure to all the counterforces that would carry it away from the lives of things; yet such critical security is gained only by inhibiting the force with which the words of such an author as Beston draw us to things in their singularity.

In this critical capacity, philosophical writing will need to insist on what Scott calls the "dimensions that are without meaning, text, or utterance in the occurrences of things" (24). Insistence is needed in order to give force to signifying operations that would declare something unsignifiable, that would mean precisely what will necessarily "withdraw from our meanings" (31). Insistence is needed at least as long as one does not—or can not—put into play the gift—more poetic than philosophic—of writing in such a way that what is said exceeds what is meant, signification thus outdistancing itself.

But beyond the insistence that would hold open the space beyond signification, something else is required, something specifically critical. For there are counterforces that tend to close off that space, making us oblivious to it and thereby concealing the singularities by which the lives of things exceed their significations. The word "nature" and its meaning can be—and indeed have been—a primary means by which such closure has been effected. This happens when "nature" is made to name very general conditions of things and thus is itself taken as unchanging and universal, as possessing coherence and inevitability. What comes to count for the lives of things are these universal, unchanging conditions that determine them, not what pertains to the singularity of each. Scott traces the consequences: "in many interpretations of 'nature,' things are detached from their own astonishing, singular, and unspeakable events: we interpret *them* by reference to something that they in their singularity are not, or are only a subsidiary part of. In that case we often know things best when we look away from them to something that is their 'essence'" (26). This is what's the matter with "nature": it blinds us to things in their singularity. Captivated by nature itself in its unchanging universality, we are drawn away from natural things, granting to those things only what accords with nature itself. This is what's wrong with "nature," and this is what philosophical critique must address, interrupt, and dismantle.

One way of doing this is to pose critically, indeed deconstructively, the question of the nature of nature. The doubling of nature in this question—say, in the question "What is the nature of nature?"—can express the positing of an idea or essence of nature beyond nature, the placing of the truth of nature beyond nature in its dispersion and its singularities. The fact that the word "nature" commonly has this double sense in the modern European languages, that it can signify both the manifold of natural things and the essence of something, even of something not natural—as when one speaks of the nature of art, for instance—attests to the force and consistency with which philosophy has determined nature precisely by projecting it beyond itself, by positing a nature beyond nature. In interrupting and dismantling this project, philosophy thus turns critically, deconstructively, against itself.

The question can then be reformulated as referring to another kind of doubling. To ask about the nature of nature would not be to ask about something beyond nature that, in its permanence and universality, would determine everything essential about natural things, while also rendering utterly insignificant whatever about the lives of things is not essential. On the contrary, it would become a matter of asking about something within nature, about a doubling of nature within nature rather than beyond nature. Scott touches on such a doubling when he translates nature back into φύσις and insists on the distinction; he says in this connection that φύσις "can name a thing's coming to be, its continuing animation and becoming" (29). Such a naming is found in Aristotle. Doubling nature by differentiating between nature and natural things—or, adhering to the Greek, between φύσις and τὰ φύσει ὄντα—Aristotle defines φύσις precisely as that within τὰ φύσει ὄντα that determines the movement, the becoming, by which such natural things are as they are. Thus defined, nature (φύσις) is neither an unchanging universal nor anything else posited beyond the natural beings it determines. It is *not any thing* at all, not something tucked away somewhere within the natural thing it determines. If one insists on asking still what it is, one will have to displace the question of the what (the question: τί ἐστι . . .?) from the determination that it was given precisely by Greek philosophy and that we express, still today, by words such as *essence*, *idea*, and indeed *nature* in the unnatural sense. With this precaution in place, one can then repeat Aristotle's answer: φύσις is an ἀρχή, the ἀρχὴ κινήσεως of τὰ φύσει ὄντα. As an ἀρχή, it is neither a nature beyond nature nor itself a natural thing or a part of a natural thing.

To be sure, the question can be raised whether Aristotle carries out this turn to the ἀχρή of natural things in a way that remains true to this intent; or whether in the affiliation that he establishes between φύσις, on the one hand, and μορφή and εἶδος, on the other, he comes around eventually to positing a nature beyond nature. My purpose in referring to this central problematic of Aristotle's *Physics* is not to venture an answer to this question, which would require going far afield from Scott's work. My purpose is rather to begin underlining the complexity of the philosophical return to an ἀρχή and the manifold itineraries open to such a return.

Scott makes a proposal in this regard, one that he explicitly marks as a hypothesis. He writes: "My hypothesis is that when people are predisposed to experience events and are relieved of a quest for definitive origins that explain why something occurs and that define its meaning from the beginning, they are more able to pay attention to the often astonishing happenings around them, happenings that never quite fit their duplications in meanings and values" (45).

To the extent that this quest is one that goes beyond the happenings of natural things and that does so definitively in the sense of taking its stance once and for all in that beyond and of regarding the happenings of things only from that stance—to this extent this hypothesis simply reaffirms the need to dismantle the nature beyond nature. Mere recourse to such intelligibles as constituting the ἀρχή of things in their happenings will never eventuate in a thinking capable of matching up to those happenings. At most it will suffice for apprehending the presence of things to us, the sense they offer up to us; but in its adherence to significations or intelligibles, such recourse will remain aloof from and blind to the unappropriable quality that installs things at a differential distance and renders their presence to us utterly volatile.

The question is whether such recourse can be sustained, that is, whether thinking can once and for all station itself in an archaic domain definitively beyond the happenings of things. Or does an unappropriable quality announce itself not only in the lives of the things that would be apprehended but also in the life of the one who would carry out the philosophical return to the ἀρχή, indeed to such an extent that it would volatize the presence of and to sheer intelligibility, establishing a differential distance that would serve precisely to draw one back toward the unappropriable happenings of things? In other words, is the would-be simple move to the ἀρχή diverted into a more complex figure? Is there not at least an inevitable recoil from the ἀρχή, a recoil that would constitute, not a failure of thinking, but a moment in the very figure of thinking? Would such a recoil perhaps open a field in which a pluralizing of ἀρχαί might unfold? For if the drive to a unique origin is interrupted, if thinking falters in its ascent toward an end that would be the beginning of everything, then, short of that one being, it would be thrown back upon a manifold. Would a pluralizing not only of ἀρχαί but of kinds of ἀρχαί break out? Suppose that one set out to think as another kind of ἀρχή the very instigation of the withdrawal of things into their singularity. Could one, then, even imagine the figure of thinking that would need to be drawn?

Certain moments at least of the figure of thinking as return to the ἀρχή are drawn in the Platonic dialogues. Such a drawing extends in the broadest of strokes throughout the *Phaedo*. In this dialogue Socrates puts forth—in a voice not his own—a conception of philosophy as devotion "to nothing else but dying and being dead" (64a). Such at least is the conception outlined near the beginning of the conversation that takes place as he awaits his own death. Philosophy would consist in dying away from the body and from all sensible things, taking flight to the intelligible εἴδη, of which sensible things are mere images. This conception reappears later in the dialogue, its Orphic-Pythagorean motifs then appearing still more extreme. Socrates depicts the soul's ascent to what is pure and always is and always is selfsame. Akin to such being as such, the soul comes to be always with it and then, in Socrates' words, "it ceases its wandering and, around those things, remains always the same in the same way, because it's touched such things" (79d).

And yet, one cannot but wonder about the state of this soul that would complete its return to selfsame intelligibility, settling in and securing itself there to such an extent as to be itself unqualifiedly selfsame. One cannot but wonder whether the state achieved would be one of thoughtfulness (φρόνησις); or whether it would be a state in which thought would simply have ceased, a state of deathlessness that could hardly be distinguished from death—death, then, as the end of philosophy, from which, short of being entirely terminated, thinking (that is, the philosopher) must undergo recoil. It is precisely this recoil of and from the ἀρχή that is in play in word or deed at virtually every stage of the *Phaedo*. It is in play from the very beginning of the conversation: sitting up, Socrates bends his recently unchained leg and begins speaking about the curious mixture of pleasure and pain. It is the body, Socrates' body, that prompts the entire conversation. It is the body that, within the drama, functions as the ἀρχή—at least as *an* ἀρχή—of the speech. Shortly after he sits up, Socrates assumes a certain posture, one that is more telling than any word could be: "And with these words, he put his feet down on the earth and for the rest of the time conversed sitting in this way" (61d). The recoil of and from the ἀρχή is played out beautifully in Socrates' last speech in the *Phaedo*. In this speech, the last he will ever give, Socrates speaks of the earth; he tells a story of the earth, sings his song of the earth. And in this swan song of swan songs even the highest region to which purified souls would ascend is depicted as an upper region *of the earth*.

These are only the very broadest strokes by which the moment of recoil is drawn in the *Phaedo*. Its more rigorous elaboration occurs in the discourse on remembrance, which binds knowing to sense images, and in the discourse governed by the figure of the second sailing, which binds thought to λόγος. Entering into these elaborations would take us too far afield, so let it suffice merely to have traced in outline this moment of recoil that belongs to the figure of thinking.

Still another moment is drawn in the *Timaeus*; Scott has touched on it in his extended discussion of the chorological stratum of this dialogue. Here again it is a matter of interrupting the ascent, an ascent that here is carried out by casting one's vision upward, gazing on the starry heaven, and instilling in oneself the orderly patterns seen above. It is precisely at the point where such vision is celebrated that Timaeus interrupts his discourse, breaks it off in order to make a new beginning. In this new beginning, in the discourse that commences from it, it is a matter of turning back from the fabrication of the cosmos as an image of the intelligible paradigm, back to what Timaeus calls the errant form of cause, errant in something like the way that a planet, compared to the fixed stars, is a wanderer. Timaeus says explicitly that it is a matter of going back and taking up a different beginning (ἑτέραν ἀρχήν). Here the word ἀρχή is submitted to one of its doublings: it is a matter of turning back so as to begin anew, to make a beginning other to the beginning made in Timaeus' previous discourse; but—and this is the other sense—this turn is carried out precisely as a turn to a different ἀρχή, to an ἀρχή other to the intelligible paradigm that serves as ἀρχή in the earlier discourse. This turn to a different ἀρχή—pluralizing the kinds of ἀρχαί—is first presented as a turn to nature, to a nature before nature. Timaeus says: "We must begin again from the beginning. We must bring into view the nature [φύσις] itself of fire and water, and air and earth, before the generation of the heaven" (48b). Both in bringing these into view and in order to bring them into view, Timaeus has to draw into the discourse something that offers no view, no look, something even more insistently invisible than the intelligible εἴδη. Timaeus calls it the third kind, different both from the intelligible kind and from the sensible kind. This other kind of ἀρχή, which eventually will be named χώρα, is, on at least one occasion, also called φύσις.[4] Everything would suggest at least that it is closer to nature and to natural things than is the nature beyond nature. The introduction of this other kind of ἀρχή fractures the sense of ἀρχή more severely than one might suppose: for, strictly speaking, the χώρα cannot even be considered a kind of ἀρχή, since the very division into kinds falls completely within the domain of the intelligible εἴδη. The χώρα is a kind of kind beyond kind, and it is this strange "beyond," utterly foreign to that of the nature beyond nature, that lays out still another moment in the figure of thinking.

Since Scott's discourse on "What's the matter with 'nature'?" engages chorology at length and in depth, I will need to return to this strangest of themes. For it is, above all, in this connection that I want to pose some questions with respect to what Scott takes to be the matter with "nature."

But, first, I need to turn back to the hypothesis—Scott's hypothesis—that by being relieved of the quest for origins one would be able to pay better attention to the happenings, the lives, of things. Now, if the quest for origins consists simply in having recourse to a nature beyond nature, transmuting nature into essence, then I suspect that Scott is entirely right. And I suspect, too, that what best attests to this truth of Scott's hypothesis are writings like those by Beston that both Scott and I cite.

Yet to accept the hypothesis in this form is something different from what Scott seems to call for in some other passages, even though these passages are in every case embedded in a context that leaves open a great deal more than one might suppose. To endorse the turn

4. Timaeus speaks of "the nature [φύσις] that receives all bodies" (*Tim.* 50b).

from the nature beyond nature back to the lives of things does not—to mention one such passage—amount to giving the simply affirmative answer that seems to be invited when Scott asks: "Are not the lives of things and the meanings that things have for us in our ordinary lives enough?" (53). This question is not the same as most of the others that directly follow it as if in apposition; it is not the same, for instance, as asking whether the ancient preoccupation with Life (capitalized) beyond lives has not today become merely optional, which is to say dispensable. Indeed the *Timaeus* itself—by launching and then interrupting a discourse that seeks to account for living things by reference to a capitalized Life, the paradigm of living being—shows that mere adherence to the ordinary lives of things is not the only alternative once the recoil by and from the nature beyond nature has been undergone. There is another passage in which Scott addresses the same theme; but this passage is more subtle, as it occurs within the context of Scott's discussion of φύσις as capable of naming a thing's coming to be, its continuing animation and becoming. Scott insists, however, that φύσις need not be regarded as providing unity nor as itself unified, and it is in this connection that he writes: "It's rather that in being what it is, *a* thing is *this* event and not any of the other events. And we stop there. No speculative explanations, no ultimate structure . . . , no thought of some 'higher' nature" (27).

The question is whether one *can* stop there. It is a question of whether there is an itinerary such that, having followed it, one would then be able, in some sense, to stop there. Simply stopping there without having somehow returned there would seem to fall short even of empiricism, which always is secretly nourished by its opposition to whatever is posited beyond the sensible. What would be required, then, in order to be able to adhere to the *there* without simply relinquishing the critical function that thinking otherwise carries out? For mere adherence to the meanings that things have for us in our ordinary lives would risk leaving these meanings intact, letting them govern our lives, however vacuous or ideological they might be. For the meanings that things seem simply and immediately to have for us are all-too-frequently constituted within a context—a social-political context, for instance—that must be exposed if we are not simply to remain submitted to them. Critique of such meanings belongs to the freedom of thought, and such critique can be carried out effectively only if the ways in which meanings are constituted are exposed and analyzed. In this respect the meanings that things have for us in our ordinary lives are not enough.

Neither, it seems to me, can one simply stop with the observation that a thing is *this* event and not any of the other events. For seldom is it the case—as the ancients well recognized—that something is just this, just itself, and not anything else, not anything other than itself. Such beings with no admixture of otherness proved so exceptional that the ancients gave them special names and distinguished them from all the others. But even to judge whether something is just this (just what it is) and not anything other requires that the sense of identity, of selfsameness, as well as of otherness, of difference, be determined. An index of what is required for such determination is provided by the analysis of the five kinds in Plato's *Sophist*. If, furthermore, there is—as with Scott—an insistence on a kind of difference that is no longer a difference of kind, on such difference as bestows upon things their unappropriable quality while distancing them and volatizing their presence with us, then the need for a rigorous determination of such difference becomes all the greater.

The turnings of thought that would be required for rigorous determination and critique would not aim at restoring some "beyond" in which the diversity and singularity of the lives of things would be overruled. This, it seems to me, is the profound truth in Scott's declaration: "And we stop there." Yet one can stop there without thereby relinquishing critique, determination, indeed philosophical thinking itself only if one returns to the *there* from out of a distance. The parameters are analogous to—though not the same as—those that Derrida outlines in referring to the transcendental critique that is necessary in order to avoid falling back into—or of course never escaping from—naive objectivism. Derrida proposes that there is "a short-of [a this-side of—*un en-deçà*] and a beyond [*un au-delà*] of transcendental critique." And because the transcendentality of that critique has also to be put in question, Derrida says that "the ultra-transcendental text will so closely resemble the precritical text as to be indistinguishable from it."[5] All that will distinguish them is the wake (*le sillage*) left in the text by the passage through critique.

5. Jacques Derrida, *De la Grammatologie* (Paris: Éditions de Minuit, 1967), 90.

In depicting the figure of thinking as a return to the ἀρχή, with all of the counterturns and doublings involved, I am referring to an itinerary that is like that on which Derrida deploys transcendental critique and yet broader, at a decisive distance from the problematic of transcendentality, even in its most rigorous, that is, Husserlian form.

It is highly appropriate that more than half of Scott's discourse "What's the Matter with 'Nature'?" is devoted to the *Timaeus*, primarily to the chorology. For it is in the turn to this other ἀρχή, so other as not even to be another *kind* of ἀρχή, that the singularity of things and the difference that bestows on them their unappropriable quality come to be. Let me stress that in this thinking it is not a matter of adding to—or beyond—singular things some other things such as a nature beyond nature that would overrule these singulars. For the ἀρχή as well as the turn to it prove to be so utterly strange that virtually everything that would be said of the nature beyond nature falls away and entirely fails to touch this third kind, which is called by several names but most properly—if one can speak here of propriety—is called the χώρα.

Some of the names that Timaeus bestows on the χώρα may suggest that it is less strange than it turns out to be once the bastardly discourse is carried through. Scott toys with suggesting that it is a kind of "transcending there" that provides the site for generation as well as for individuation. This is not false, though extreme caution is required with a word as overloaded with all the wrong senses as *transcending* and *transcendent*. But indeed Timaeus does speak of the χώρα as providing an abode (ἕδρα) for things; yet it is decisive that in furnishing an abode for things, the χώρα also imparts to them errancy. And yet, lest one come to rest in the image of the χώρα as a kind of place, the nurse or womb of all things, one needs to observe that different images of the χώρα collide and are even mutually disruptive; since no image can be adequate to the χώρα, it could not be otherwise. And so, alongside—indeed against—the topical images of the χώρα, there is the image of it as the gold that can be modeled into all possible figures or shapes. The χώρα may indeed carry "powerful overtones of a kind of place" (51), but it is neither a kind nor a place nor place as such. Even if Timaeus does allow that in dreams we often conflate χώρα and τόπος.

Toward the end of his discussion of the χώρα, Scott poses mere emptiness over against what he calls the fecundity of the χώρα. Here he is very much on the lookout for theological strategies for avoiding emptiness, strategies for avoiding the void. His question becomes in effect: What's the matter with the void?—or, as he asks explicitly: What is so bad about mere void? Let me be perfectly clear: he does not say that the chorology is a strategy for avoiding the void nor that it would thus be entirely dispensable, should one decide that the mere void is not so bad after all. But he does set the χώρα and the void in a certain opposition, and, by declaring the χώρα, as he says, "unspeakably plenteous and immeasurably rich in generosity" (52), he hints that the chorology may not be entirely free of affiliation with the force of resistance to void and emptiness.

Perhaps it is not. And perhaps there is no reason why one should expect it not to be, for it is hardly to be taken for granted that resistance to void runs counter to thinking or that bold affirmation of utter emptiness attests to rigorous thinking.

In any case it seems to me that there is an answer to the question Scott in effect poses, the question "What's the matter with mere void?" The answer I would suggest is that, when used with such generality, the void is the mere symmetrical opposite to full presence and that for this reason there is the danger that the appeal to it continues to be controlled by this opposition and thus by the metaphysical value of presence. Yet, however this may be, in the *Timaeus* the void (τὸ κενόν) is taken up in the account of the elements and of their interactions in which the voids internal to them play a significant role (see 58b). The entire account is situated at a stage where the mere traces in the χώρα have been separated and given the shapes of regular solids; clearly, then, the constitution of voids presupposes the χώρα rather than representing a primordial alternative to it. The χώρα does not bring fullness to a void; rather a void can be generated only if the χώρα is already in force.

Is it clear even that the χώρα is plenteous and rich in generosity? What does its hospitality really amount to beyond receiving and holding all things? For the only gift it bestows on sensible things is the gift of being; more precisely, it gives such things the wherewithal to cling to being in a certain way so as to avoid being nothing at all. The χώρα allows these things, which are utterly removed from being itself, nevertheless somehow to be. A great gift, no doubt. But not a gift that is plenteous, not a gift of presence and fullness. Rather the gift that allows them only to cling somehow to being.

The chorology is thus an affirmation of sensible things as being without being. It is an affirmation of the lives of things in all that sets them apart from being itself, an affirmation of them and of their unappropriable quality and differential distance from the sense offered to us.

So then: What's the matter with "nature"? Scott's answer is forceful and compelling, and my intention has been primarily to underline and here and there to amplify this answer. What is wrong with "nature" is that it denotes, not nature, not the natural lives of things but the nature beyond nature, which overrules things and reduces their unappropriable quality. One could add that a primary instrument for carrying out this reduction is the word ὕλη, which has the effect of keeping nature at the limit of being.[6] This is the word that, with Aristotle, came to replace χώρα, before then being translated into "*materia*" and "matter." Thus one could also say that matter is what's the matter with nature.

And yet, if the question "What's the matter with nature?" were to be posed again, now within the context of the *Timaeus*, still another answer would be possible. For all that's wrong with nature, its deviations and irregularities, its gaps and discontinuities, even the insufficiencies of living things and the illnesses and diseases to which their insufficiencies expose them—all of this only testifies to the errant workings of the χώρα, to the traces that it leaves amidst things of sense. Thus in this context one could answer the question "What's the matter with nature?" with the single word χώρα.

---

6. See my *Force of Imagination: The Sense of the Elemental* (Bloomington: Indiana University Press, 2000), 149.

CHAPTER 8

TRAGEDY FROM AFAR

WHAT COUNTS IS distance.

What counts is how distance is measured, measured out, counted out, counted off.

This is what counts in the case of legacies, for example. Also in the case of tragedy.

In Book 10 of the *Republic* Socrates broaches both subjects, broaches them together. It is a matter of the Homeric legacy, of recognizing this legacy while restraining the honor accorded it. Socrates says of Homer: "For he seems to have been the first teacher and leader of all these beautiful tragic things. Still and all, a man must not be honored before the truth, but, as I say, it must be told" (595c). What is it that—as Socrates says with the force of a performative—must be told? What must be told is the truth that is to be honored even above Homer. What must be told is the truth about tragedy, about the legacy of tragedy.

As he is about to tell this truth, indeed as the final step leading to it, Socrates introduces a curious description of those whom he calls imitators (μιμητής). The imitator, he says, is one who is "of the third generation from nature [τοῦ τρίτου . . . γεννήματος ἀπὸ τῆς φύσεως]" (597e). One thing that is curious about this description is that it pertains primarily to the imitator and not directly to what is generated by imitation, by means of the imitative τέχνη practiced by the imitator. It seems that the imitator has himself to be generated at this distance from nature in order then, through his μιμητική, to generate those imitations that will also themselves prove to be set at such a distance. Only from afar, so it would seem, can the imitator generate those phantoms (εἴδωλα)—namely, paintings and tragedies—that are themselves remote from the works of the true τεχνίτης and still more remote from nature itself, from "what is itself in nature" (598a). Thus imitation involves a double distancing from nature, a distancing both of the imitator and of the imitation produced.

There is also something else about this description that is curious, something strange about the way the distance is measured, about the direction in which it is counted out. The generation to which both imitator and imitation are submitted does not occur within nature; it is not a generating according to nature, as parents beget children. Rather, it is a generation away from nature (ἀπὸ τῆς φύσεως), a generation that distances from nature, that sets what is generated three generations away from nature. Imitation thus puts in play an order of generation that with respect to nature is an order of degeneration.

To Socrates' description of imitators, which he poses as a question, Glaucon answers: "Most certainly [πάνυ μὲν οὖν]." With the truth of imitation thus established, the truth of tragedy can now, it seems, be told. Abandoning the interrogative form, Socrates declares: "Therefore this will also apply to the maker of tragedy, if he is an imitator; he is naturally third from king and from the truth, as are all the other imitators" (597e). Even though Socrates has told—that is, declared rather than asked about—the truth of tragedy, Glaucon's response is more reserved. He says: "Probably [κινδυνεύει]"—or, more literally: it is to be ventured, risked (κίνδυνος means *venture*, *risk*, *danger*). In this response there is hesitation, even though what Socrates has declared seems to be nothing more than an extension of the description that Glaucon has just affirmed as most certain; the transition to the truth of tragedy seems only to require agreeing that tragedians are imitators. Yet the hesitation never quite disappears: the entire discussion concludes by holding open the possibility of retraction, by insisting that if poetry should deliver a λόγος showing its worthiness to exist in the city, then it should be received back from the exile to which the charges of degeneration would have condemned it (see 607c). Why the hesitation? Why does Socrates hold open the possibility of an apology by which poetry—in particular, tragedy—would redeem itself? One cannot but suspect that the hesitation, which first appears with the move from imitation in general to tragedy in particular, is linked to the love (φιλία) of Homer and the shame or reverence (αἰδώς) before him that Socrates confesses at the outset. It is a matter of the Homeric legacy, a matter of remaining, conditionally, from afar, open to that legacy.

But what about the truth of tragedy? As with imitators in general, what counts is distance. Both tragedian and tragedy are thrice removed from king and from the truth. Generated in an order that leads away from nature, the tragedian falls outside the royal line and has no claim to the legacy that is passed along in the order of natural generation. Both tragedian and tragedy are thrice removed from the truth: the truth of tragedy is that it is distant from the truth, and the truth of the tragedian is at best a truth apprehended from afar. Yet what is most remarkable about the truth of the tragedian as told by Socrates is that this distance, this remoteness, is something natural, that the tragedian is naturally (πεφυκώς) thrice removed from king, from the truth, and, as with all imitators, from nature. One will hesitate therefore to say simply that the order of tragedy is one of degeneration from nature. Rather, as determined by a distancing from nature that is itself natural, by a natural removal from nature, tragedian and tragedy are monstrous. The truth of tragedy is its monstrosity.

All that Socrates declares or asks about the Homeric legacy of tragedy is set within the compass of this truth, this unveiling of tragedy. From the various complexes of discourse, let me extract three that are especially pertinent.

In the first, Socrates draws a contrast between the kind of character that lends itself to presentation in tragedy and an opposite kind. Tragedy favors the character that is irritable (ἀγανακτητικόν) and changeful or manifold (ποικίλον), since this kind is easily imitated and its imitation is satisfying to the many who attend the theatre. On the other hand, Socrates speaks as advocate of another kind of character, one whom he designates as fitting or reasonable (ἐπιεικής). This is the kind of character who, suffering some calamity, "will bear it more easily than others" (603e). While one who is of such character will be drawn by suffering to his pain, λόγος and ordinance (νόμος) will dictate that he hold out, that he not give in to his pain. He will thus be capable of taking his distance, accepting the calamity and recognizing that the good and the bad in such things are not manifest. Such a prudent and quiet character (τὸ . . . φρόνιμον τε καὶ ἡσύχιον ἦθος) is neither easily imitated nor, when imitated, is it easily understood by the many at the theatre.

The second discourse comes near the beginning of Book 10, just after the reference to Homer and long before the truth of tragedy comes to be told. It is the discourse by which Socrates first introduces the theme of imitation and, in particular, the imitator, the one who practices the τέχνη of imitation (μιμητική). Socrates speaks of a certain craftsman (δημιουργός), one apart from all others. This craftsman is one who makes everything that the other artisans make separately. Socrates elaborates: this craftsman "is not only able to make all implements but also makes everything that grows naturally from the earth, and he produces all living beings, the others and himself too, and, in addition to that, produces earth and heaven and gods and everything in heaven and everything in Hades under the earth" (596c). Glaucon exclaims at this "wonderful sophist" of whom Socrates speaks. Yet his incredulity dissolves as Socrates goes on to explain to Glaucon how he too could make all these things: "you could craft them quickly in many ways and most quickly if you are willing to take a mirror and carry it around everywhere; quickly you will make the sun and the things in the heaven, quickly the earth, and quickly yourself and the other living beings and implements and plants and everything else that was just now mentioned" (596d–e). What is remarkable—and yet goes unremarked as Socrates and Glaucon move on toward identifying this craftsman as the imitator—is that the only other thing "that was just now mentioned" but that is omitted in the passage about the mirror is "everything in Hades under the earth." Yet everything in Hades (Ἅιδης) is concealed under the earth. It cannot be seen by living beings, is unseeable, invisible (ἀειδής) to them, as the assonance between Ἅιδης and ἀειδής suggests. In particular, the things of Hades could not be seen by the wonderful sophist carrying the mirror around, and consequently an image of these things could not be caught in the mirror. Unlike all other things, the things in Hades do not submit to imitation. This dark, shadowy realm inhabited by the souls of the dead and withdrawn utterly from the living is not to be seen and thus also cannot be submitted to imitation. Despite the way in which most, if not all, Greek tragedy is gathered around death, around discourse on death, the realm to which one passes after death would be—granted Socrates' example—utterly resistant to tragic representation. Death would mark the limit of tragedy; and even if the words of the poet conjure up the shades of Hades (as in Book 23 of the *Odyssey*), these shades nonetheless withdraw beyond the limit of tragic representation. If, as Socrates has said, tragedy deals only with phantoms, its phantoms make no contact with those said to inhabit the underworld.

The third discourse, near the end of the entire discussion, broaches for a brief moment the subject of comedy. Socrates refers to a certain propensity to laughter that is within each of us but that we suppress for fear of being reputed a buffoon; the case of laughter parallels closely in this respect that of the reasonable man, of whom Socrates spoke earlier, the one able to maintain his distance from—that is, to suppress—the preoccupation with pain. But now Socrates' point is that when the previously suppressed propensity to laughter is released, then one gets carried away in domestic matters, carried away with household affairs (ἐν τοῖς οἰκείοις), so that one becomes a comic poet. Despite the tone of censure in this passage, Socrates does not say that one ought not be so carried away; neither does he draw attention to the peculiar directionality of this comic motion, that it involves being carried away from oneself in a way that engages one precisely in what is one's own, in one's household. Indeed one would hardly expect Socrates to condemn such ecstatic laughter, considering that precisely when, much earlier in the *Republic*, the discussion turned to women and children, Socrates and Glaucon were themselves carried away into the enactment of a comedy.[1]

Let it suffice for the moment to note one thing that is accomplished by these three discourses linked to the telling of the truth of tragedy. These discourses outline the figure of another truth set obliquely at a distance from the monstrosity of tragedy. It is the figure of an enactment posed at the threshold of death, of an enactment by one capable of taking his distance from the impending calamity, one capable of remaining almost reasonable, prudent, and quiet in the face of an event that would evoke tragic pathos in the hearts of others. Yet it is also an enactment that is not entirely lacking in laughter and comedy.

▼ ● ◆

In taking up, from the side of philosophy, the relation between philosophy and tragedy, Dennis Schmidt is keenly aware of the perils of omitting comedy. He notes even that when poetry has been addressed

1. See *Being and Logos*, 371–78.

to philosophy, this has been "done so much more frequently in the form of comedy," and, above all, by Aristophanes. Thus Schmidt grants that a "full treatment of the relation of tragedy and philosophy . . . needs to address the place of comedy in that relation."[2]

Yet comedy is not Schmidt's concern, nor need it have been, granted the project he sets out. *On Germans and Other Greeks* is a work that crystallizes a history, rendering it for the first time visible in its integrity, yet also with the enigmatic shadows that it casts, the questions that it leaves open or that it knots together into quandaries that thinking has still to confront. This hitherto untold history is that of the relation—often, as in Plato, a troubled relation—between tragedy and philosophy. Though this history begins with Plato and Aristotle (the "Other Greeks" of the title) and though Schmidt addresses the relevant discussions in the *Republic* and the *Poetics*, the primary concern of his work is with the renewal and reappropriation of the question of tragedy in post-Kantian German philosophy. In German philosophy from Schelling on, it is a matter of appropriating tragedy—or rather, what can now be called *the tragic*—for philosophical thinking itself, for philosophical thinking especially as it is driven to engage the question of the end of philosophy, the question that, though in various registers, is shared by all these philosophers. As Schmidt formulates it: "At the very moment the question of the end of philosophy came to prominence the topic of tragedy—not taken as a specialized literary genre but as a way of asking about ends, destiny, and history—comes forward as a sort of model for asking and answering the questions of such times" (G, 6). Precisely at the end of philosophy these philosophers turn back to the tragic art that preceded the beginning of philosophy; these Germans turn back to Greek tragedy in order to find the resources with which to think this end, taking up the end by going back more deeply into the Greek beginning, philosophically appropriating tragedy from afar.

On Germans and Other Greeks traces—renders visible—the history of this reappropriation of the tragic for thinking at the end of philosophy. Schmidt begins with the Kantian background: the antinomy of reason in the first Critique, which tragic conflict will be taken to mirror; the recovery of art for ethical life in the third Cri-

2. Dennis J. Schmidt, *On Germans and Other Greeks: Tragedy and Ethical Life* (Bloomington: Indiana University Press, 2001), 19. Subsequent references are given in the text as G.

tique; and, also in the third Critique, the development of the concept of the sublime by which, as Schmidt says, "Kant created a place for the philosophical discussion of the presentations of the monstrous and sacrifice which are so central to Greek tragedy" (G, 75). But Schelling is still more decisive in this regard. Schmidt pinpoints in Schelling's Tenth Letter on Dogmatism and Criticism the appeal to Greek tragedy as showing how thinking can endure the most extreme contradiction, how the contradiction between freedom and necessity posed in Kant's Third Antinomy can be engaged by thinking rather than simply repelling it. In this connection one might recall a passage from Hegel's *Aesthetics* that underlines just how central the engagement with contradiction is for German Idealism: "Whoever demands that nothing exist that carries in itself a contradiction in the form of an identity of opposites is at the same time requiring that nothing living exist. For the force of life, and still more the power of the spirit, consists precisely in positing contradiction in itself, enduring it, and overcoming it."[3] For the thinking of Schelling and Hegel, it is Greek tragedy above all that shows how contradiction is to be thus endured and overcome. The highest demand placed upon such thinking is, in Schmidt's words, "to grasp the tragedy of spirit speculatively, that is, as a unity which is a unity precisely because it is lodged in the antinomy of its own contradictions" (G, 90).

The history of the philosophical appropriation of the tragic continues with Hölderlin. Schmidt shows how the question of tragedy frames Hölderlin's work as a whole, not only his translations of Sophocles and his attempts to write a modern tragedy under the title *The Death of Empedocles* but also the more purely theoretical discussions in various texts and letters. The bond with German Idealism is demonstrated by Hölderlin's assertion that tragedy is "the metaphor of an intellectual intuition" and that through this metaphor tragedy places one at the site of pure speculative identity, where the oppositions between thought and intuition and between subject and object would be surpassed. And yet, it is of the utmost consequence that tragedy is only the metaphor, not the accomplishment, of intellectual intuition; for it is as such that it can also turn into the rupture of the speculative, the caesura, as Hölderlin calls it. It is, then, this double move,

3. G. W. F. Hegel, *Ästhetik*, ed. Friedrich Bassenge (Westberlin: das europäische buch, 1985), 1:125.

this intrinsically conflicted gesture that tragedy presents to philosophy: "Here the very same gesture which will resolve the divisions of life will rend life" (G, 123). Yet this move back into tragedy is not only theorized but also enacted, as in Hölderlin's translations of *Oedipus Tyrannos* and *Antigone*, translations so radical and creative that, as Schmidt puts it, "Hölderlin's ambitions in these translations is . . . to teach the German language to speak Greek" (G, 150).

The penultimate phase of the history occurs with Nietzsche, primarily in *The Birth of Tragedy*. Schmidt emphasizes that in this work the two principal strands of Nietzsche's early thought are systematically woven together. On the one hand, there is the analysis of Greek tragedy in terms of the monstrous opposition of Apollinian and Dionysian, that is, the portrayal of Greek tragedy as the Apollinian dream-image of Dionysian music projected from the chorus onto the scene of the drama. On the other hand, *The Birth of Tragedy* already broaches the critique of contemporary life and culture that will become ever more shrill in Nietzsche's later writings; what is distinctive about the form that this critique takes in *The Birth of Tragedy* is that it is linked to the account Nietzsche gives of the death of tragedy at the hands of Euripides, who, in turn, is little more than a mask for Socrates.

Against the background of Schmidt's discussion, it should be stressed that Nietzsche sets Socrates—or at least the so-called Socratism that speaks through him—in utter opposition to tragedy. In Nietzsche's view—at least up to a point—it is a matter of direct conflict between the Socratic demand for unlimited uncovering and the tragic art that leaves the depths concealed beneath shining images. By prevailing over tragedy, by expelling it, Socrates initiated—according to Nietzsche—a decline the history of which virtually coincides with the history of philosophy itself. Only in what Nietzsche could have called the end of philosophy, namely, that marking of the limit of Socratism that begins with Kant, does there arise the prospect of a rebirth of tragedy.

It is only in this connection that Nietzsche shifts from the near-caricature to a more nuanced sense of the Platonic Socrates, specifically of the Socrates of the *Phaedo*. No longer setting Socrates simply in opposition to tragedy, Nietzsche even goes so far as to cast the coming rebirth of tragedy in the figure of the music-practicing Socrates. This is the point where everything again becomes questionable, where, above all, one cannot evade the question of just how, if indeed at all, the Socratic or at least a trace of the Socratic would belong to the rebirth of tragedy that Nietzsche finds portended. Who would the music-practicing Socrates be? Even if one is content to say he is Zarathustra, still it needs to be asked: What moments would be consolidated in this figure? In other words, how would philosophy *in its end* belong to the very rebirth of the tragic that would thus be made possible?

Schmidt traces the history to its end with Heidegger. One gets the sense that there is something unusual—not to say provocative—about the way Heidegger takes up the theme of tragedy. For instance, Schmidt hesitates even to suggest that there is a theory of tragedy to be found in Heidegger, noting that all Heidegger's discussions of tragedy are embedded in contexts devoted to other themes and that, rather than explicitly developing a theory of tragedy, these discussions seem to rely on an understanding of tragedy that remains largely unformulated. For Heidegger tragedy has to do, above all, with the power of history; what Greek tragedy explores and unfolds is the necessity that history puts in force, the work of destiny. Over against the conception of the human being as a subject, tragedy portrays the human as δεινόν, as fundamentally strange. Deconstructing the human as subject, Heidegger appeals to tragedy as attesting to the destiny that belongs to the nature of the mortal being, as attesting that mortals are subject to destiny.

Something else that Schmidt notes as being unusual about Heidegger's treatment of tragedy is that it is limited to only a few texts, all composed in the period between 1933 and 1946; Schmidt does not leave unexamined the fact that Heidegger's concern with tragedy thus began with the *Rectoral Address* and ended just after the end of the Second World War. It is much to Schmidt's credit that he confronts the question of Heidegger's involvement with National Socialism without resorting to the all-too-easy answers one way or another that only leave the riddle as intact as ever. Schmidt says, near the end of his account of Heidegger and tragedy, broaching the question of Heidegger *as* tragic: "And now we face another riddle, one very much about human errancy and blindness: how are we to understand how it is that one of the great minds of our times could be blind to something so decisive in his own times?" (G, 266).

Schmidt suggests also that Heidegger's apparent abandonment of the theme of tragedy after 1946 resulted from his coming to regard the distress of the present age as so deep that even tragedy fails to provide sufficient resources, that even tragedy falls short of offering what is needed in order for thinking to confront those features of the present age that Heidegger's *Contributions to Philosophy* designates by such expressions as *Seinsverlassenheit*, *Machenschaft*, and *das Riesenhafte*. The space of Heidegger's later thought would open, then, beyond the history of the philosophical appropriation of tragedy. With Heidegger that history would have come to its decisive end.

Such is, then, the history that Schmidt traces in *On Germans and Other Greeks*, the history of the linkages between philosophy and tragedy. Initially, in Plato and Aristotle, it is a matter of philosophical interrogation of tragedy. Then, in post-Kantian German philosophy it becomes a matter of appropriating tragedy for the sake of philosophical questioning as such, a matter of taking up tragedy from afar, from the distance measured out by a legacy inseparable from Platonism. The history comes to its end with Heidegger, whose thought opens beyond the legacy of philosophy and tragedy while also retreating toward a thinking anterior to philosophy. In narrating this history, Schmidt does not just tell a story, alongside which others could also be told. Rather, he displays, he demonstrates, this history in its proper integrity.

And yet, suppose one were to return to the beginning of this history. Suppose one were to turn back to the Platonic interrogation of tragedy from out of the history of philosophy and tragedy that Schmidt has so exquisitely traced. Could one still justify setting the Platonic Socrates in diametrical opposition to tragedy? Even Nietzsche, even in *The Birth of Tragedy*, had finally to let the figure of such sheer opposition mutate into that of the music-practicing Socrates. And even Nietzsche saw in Socrates a true monstrosity, even if, as he put it, "a true monstrosity per defectum" (III 1: 86).

Hegel, on the other hand, completely dissolves the opposition. For him Socrates is indeed a tragic figure. In the *Lectures on the History of Philosophy*, Hegel writes that "the fate of Socrates is genuinely tragic." He explains: "Universal moral, tragic fate lies in the arising of one right against another—not as though only one were right and the other not. Rather, both are right, are opposed, and one is shattered against the other; both suffer loss [*kommen in Verlust*], and so both are also justified over against each other. The Athenian people had themselves come to the point where the individual consciousness separates itself as independent of the universal spirit and becomes for itself; they observed this in Socrates (they were right, he also) but felt nonetheless that this was corruptive; thus they punished their own moment." Socrates is thus for Hegel the tragic hero who must perish in face of the conflict with Athens. Hegel continues: "Socrates is the hero in that he has recognized and expressed the higher principle of the spirit. This higher principle has absolute justification. But in emerging, it necessarily appears in relation to another form of spiritual consciousness that constitutes the substance of Athenian life, of the world in which Socrates emerges." The tragedy is as much that of Athens as it is of Socrates. Both will succumb to the conflict, and it is from their ashes that a higher form will arise.[4]

▼ ● ◆

The *Phaedo* has all the makings of a tragedy, and Socrates, portrayed as he faces the death to which his conflict with Athens has condemned him, has all the makings of a tragic figure. No less so, it seems, than does *Antigone* and its heroine in her conflict with Creon, a conflict between family and city, between οἶκος and νόμος, economy and law.

And yet, the *Phaedo* is not quite a tragedy, nor is the Socrates of the *Phaedo* simply a tragic figure.

Even before Phaedo sets about narrating to Echecrates the story of Socrates' last day, he begins in effect differentiating the story from tragedy. He speaks of the wondrous pathos he felt in the presence of the events of that day, and he remarks, in particular, that "no pity overcame me, even though I was present at the death of a man who was my companion" (58e). Yet pity (ἔλεος) is precisely what—according to Socrates' account in the *Republic* (see 606a–b)—is evoked by the typical scenes of tragic drama. If it appears therefore that Phaedo, witnessing the events, was more like the reasonable man, the one who remains prudent and quiet in the face of calamity, this is even more apparent in the case of Socrates himself, not just at the moment he drinks the φάρμακον, but throughout the entire conversation, in the orientation of that conversation toward charming away the fear of death.

As he is about to begin narrating the story, Phaedo recalls also the mixed condition in which all those present found themselves. They were, says Phaedo, "sometimes laughing, sometimes weeping" (59a). Theirs was a wondrous pathos, not simply the pathos of tragedy.

4. Hegel, *Vorlesungen über die Geschichte der Philosophie I* (Frankfurt a.M.: Suhrkamp, 1971), 514.

In the *Phaedo*, too, what counts is distance. Phaedo's narration of the conversation that took place in Socrates' prison cell on the day of his death is set at a distance from the event itself. Phaedo narrates the story to Echecrates in the city of Phlius, a small, somewhat isolated city in the Pelopennesus, a city known to have been a center of Pythagoreanism. Furthermore, Phaedo's λόγος—indeed that of the *Phaedo* itself—is set at a temporal distance from the events of which it tells. Since Phaedo was present when these events took place, there will have intervened at least the time—considerable, no doubt—required for him to travel from Athens to the Pelopennesus and to cross the high mountains that surround the city of Phlius.

Thus Phaedo tells of these events from afar. Beyond the opening conversation between Phaedo and Echecrates, almost the entire *Phaedo* consists of Phaedo's narrative about Socrates' last day. The two occasions when the narrative is interrupted and the dialogue with Echecrates resumed (88c–89a, 102a) serve precisely as reminders that the narrative, Phaedo's λόγος, is distanced from the events of which it tells. These two interruptions serve also to delimit the λόγος with which the dialogue attains, in philosophical significance, its pinnacle. In the interval between the interruptions, Socrates presents two λόγοι in behalf of λόγος, first, a defense against misology and then, more significantly, a discourse on how he came to philosophize as he does, on how he came to launch—as he calls it—his second sailing. In launching his second sailing—as in the absence of wind sailors take to the oars—Socrates carries out the decisive turn by which a new beginning is inaugurated. In this move he turns away from things, takes distance from them, and does so precisely by turning to λόγοι, by having recourse to them. On his second sailing he forgoes directly investigating things as well as their causes and instead, taking refuge in λόγοι, "looks in them for the truth of beings" (99e). Thus the form of the *Phaedo*, that of a λόγος set at a distance from the things of which it speaks, matches perfectly the figure of the second sailing that is drawn at the high-point of the dialogue.

The same kind of distancing, from things to λόγος, is carried out in the scene depicted by Phaedo's narrative, the scene of Socrates' last day. It is this distancing that effects the decisive differentiation of that scene from the scene of tragedy.

At the outset of the dialogue, as soon as Echecrates has ascertained that Phaedo was present on Socrates' last day, he asks: "Well, so what is it the man said before his death? And how did he die?" (57a). Thus Phaedo is to report two aspects of the scene: Socrates' approaching and meeting his death, living through the pathos of such an event; and the speeches that Socrates gives before his death, precisely as he was living through that pathos. After Phaedo has explained to Echecrates how the execution came to be delayed because of the embassy to Delos (another of the many sailings that haunt the *Phaedo*), Echecrates poses the same question again, in anticipation of Phaedo's narrative: "What happened at his death, Phaedo? What things were said and done?" (58c).

In a tragedy, too, as in the *Phaedo*, there are both things done and things said. The tragic figure lives through the conflict and suffers the impending of death wrought by the conflict. The tragic figure also—indeed, above all—speaks, and it is primarily through what is said that the pathos is made manifest. Yet it is precisely the expressiveness of tragic speech that renders it distinctive. It is a speech that expresses the tragic pathos, a speech that exposes the suffering in such a way as to lend it manifest intensity and to evoke therefore corresponding pathos in those who witness the tragic scene.

In the *Phaedo*, on the other hand, the speech—especially that of Socrates himself—is not expressive in this sense. When it tends in this direction, as with Xanthippe at the beginning and with all Socrates' companions once he has drunk the potion, Socrates interrupts and sends away or shames whoever would thus give voice to tragic pathos. It is against such soundings that Socrates says, near the end, that "one should meet one's end in propitious silence" (117e). Not long before, he has conspicuously mocked the tragic hero, feigning expression of tragic pathos and conjoining it with the need to go off to the bath: "'But me destiny calls anon,' as a man in a tragedy might declaim, and the hour for me to turn to the bath is nearly come" (115a).

Long before Socrates tells (in the discourse on the second sailing) of the discursive distancing from things, his speech has already—indeed from the outset—taken such distance. What Socrates says on the day of his death does not express, as in tragedy, the pathos of tragic suffering. But neither, in the face of death, can he quite assume the stance of the reasonable, prudent, quiet man whom in the *Republic* Socrates sets diametrically opposed to the tragic figure. On the contrary, he speaks incessantly and betrays also that he does not entirely lack the pathos that impending death evokes. Yet in what he says, through his λόγοι, he distances himself from this pathos and sets himself obliquely at a distance from the monstrosity of tragedy.

The Socrates of the *Phaedo* is no tragic figure, and even on his last day philosophy does not mutate into tragedy. But neither does the philosopher remain entirely apart, quite other than the tragic figure. In the *Phaedo* Socrates proves to be—as Nietzsche said, even if with a different intent—a true monstrosity. In the face of death the philosopher speaks in such a way as to measure out distance; and to the events and pathos that otherwise would go to make up tragedy, he comports himself from afar.

INDEX

GREEK INDEX